£8.50   5569

Spotlight on
Possums

A pair of sugar gliders licking and nuzzling one another.

Spotlight on Possums

by

Rupert Russell

Illustrated by Kay Russell

 University of Queensland Press

Typeset by Press Etching Pty Ltd, Brisbane
Printed and bound by Southwood Press Pty Ltd, Sydney

Distributed in the United Kingdom, Europe, the Middle East,
Africa, and the Caribbean by Prentice-Hall International,
International Book Distributors Ltd, 66 Wood Lane End,
Hemel Hempstead, Herts., England

National Library of Australia
Cataloguing-in-Publication data

Russell, Rupert Anley William, 1939-
  Spotlight on possums.

  Index
  Bibliography
  ISBN 0 7022 1478 7

  1. Ring-tailed phalangers. I. Russell, Kay, illus.
  II. Title.

599.2

Dedicated to enhancing an appreciation
of the Australian bushlands

Contents

Illustrations

Foreword

I first met Rupert and Kay Russell not long after they had arrived in Herberton from Mount Isa. At the time they little realized they would be writing a book on possums. Up to that time their wildlife interests had centred on reptiles. This was not surprising since reptiles abound in the dry rocky country around Mount Isa, whereas possums are seemingly absent.

Rupert expressed an interest in my study of the possums of the northern rainforests, and was soon accompanying me on many of my nocturnal forays into the mountainous ranges in the vicinity of Herberton. He even agreed to forego the pleasure of smoking his pipe until we had finished our observations for the night.

Our approaches to possum-watching were essentially different; mine as an objective scientist and Rupert as a hedonist. He would tease me, because while I had to stop watching a possum in order to take notes, he could watch continuously since he was there for the pleasure alone. This difference of approach enhanced the enjoyment of our outings, and we each learnt from the other.

By the time that I was transferred from Atherton to Townsville, Rupert's knowledge of the possums was such that he became my official honorary assistant, capturing and temporarily housing possums for me.

Kay rarely came with us on our nocturnal outings, the demands of motherhood keeping her at home. Rupert, however, was soon photographing possums for her to draw, and she was able to watch the captive animals. There were many nights when we returned to find her hunched over a drawing at the kitchen table, the Tilley lamp hissing (electricity is only a recent acquisition) as she painstakingly built up a drawing with thousands of fine dots applied with a 0.18 mm pen. For this book she has altered her technique, from dots to less laborious fine lines, using a 0.13 mm nib, but examples of her earlier style can be found in their book

A Lake in the Forest, published by Hisine Technique Ltd, Herberton, 1976.

By coming to Herberton, the Russells quite fortuitously chose the best place in Australia to study possums and gliders. Twelve of Australia's twenty-four species can be found in the vicinity of Herberton. Nowhere else in Australia, except for the neighbouring towns of Atherton, Mareeba, and Ravenshoe, could one hope to find so many species within an evening's spotlighting distance.

In the rainforest on the ranges immediately to the east of Herberton are three ringtail possums that are unique to northeastern Queensland. They are the green, Herbert River and lemur-like ringtails, predominantly leaf-eaters, that are restricted to the upland rainforests of the Townsville — Cooktown region. Of the three, the green ringtail has the most extensive range with records of its occurrence from the Paluma Range, northwest of Townsville, to the Mount Windsor Tableland, northwest of Mossman. It is also the species that is found at the lowest altitude, though not below about two hundred and fifty metres. The Herbert River ringtail has a similar range from Mount Lee, southwest of Ingham to Thornton peak, north of the Daintree River, but comes no lower than about three hundred metres in altitude, while the stronghold of the lemur-like ringtail is the range tops, where it is the most common possum between the Herbert River in the south and Kuranda in the north.

Two other rainforest possums also occur in New Guinea. One is the striped possum, which has been recorded from the Paluma Range northwards to the tip of Cape York Peninsula at all altitudes. The other is the long-tailed pigmy possum which has been recorded from the Paluma Range to Helenvale, near Cooktown, but not further north on Cape York Peninsula.

The remaining two possums to be found in the Herberton Range are species which also occur in open eucalypt forests. The coppery brushtail possum is a variety of the common brushtail, but is slightly redder and heavier, and is found in the more westerly parts of the rainforest between Atherton and the Herbert River Gorge. The sugar glider, however, is more widely distributed in the rainforest of eastern Australia and it and the striped possum are the only two possums found in the lowland rainforests of the coast to the southeast of Herberton.

All the open euaclypt forest species (the five gliders, the common brushtail, and the common ringtail) of the Herberton district are widely distributed. Herberton is, however, close to the northern limit of three of the gliders; that of the squirrel and the greater gliders near Mareeba, and of the fluffy glider on Mount Windsor Tableland. The fluffy glider has a very patchy distribution and this northern population is separated by about 760 kilometres from the next known population to the south in the vicinity of Rockhampton.

The rediscovery of the fluffy glider in northeastern Queensland, as told in this book, was one of the most exciting moments in my years of watching possums. It also shows how valuable observations by local naturalists can be, and how the first sighting of an animal can quickly lead to further sightings as one's ability to read the signs improves.

Finally, a word about common names. They should be unambiguous, easy to articulate and acceptable. It is also preferable, though not imperative, that the one common name is used for the animal throughout the range. *Hemibelideus lemuroides* has been known by two common names, the "lemur-like" and the "brush-tipped ringtail", both descriptive names, but the latter is so easy to confuse with the brushtail possum, especially when shortened forms are used in conversation, that "lemur-like" is recommended. The Russells have chosen to change "lemur-like" to "lemuroid" because the latter is more euphonious — one of the hallmarks of a good common name. The name "striped ringtail" which has sometimes been used for the green ringtail (*Pseudocheirus archeri*) is too easily confused with "striped possum" (*Dactylopsila trivirgata*). The fact that the Russells use "green possum" rather than the more widely used "green ringtail" is immaterial since there is no doubt as to which possum is concerned. Similarly the use of "feather-tail glider" rather than "pigmy glider" for *Acrobates pygmeus* is preferable in order to avoid confusion with the pigmy possums of the genus *Cercartetus*. Another departure from common practice is the use of "fluffy glider", a name first suggested by David Fleay, for the "yellow bellied glider" (*Petaurus australis*) because many individuals, particularly in the north, lack the yellow colouring.

Many of the observations on the natural history of the northern possums have been recorded for the first time in such a manner that the book will appeal to both the interested amateur and to the scientist. *Spotlight on Possums* I am sure, will be welcomed, and Kay's drawings will be a constant source of delight.

J. W. WINTER
December 1978

Introduction

A beam of light from a torch is reflected by the eyes of many animals. This enables one to locate nocturnal animals when they would otherwise be difficult to find and watch.

The forests of the Atherton Tablelands are inhabited by several species of possum, which have been the central attraction for me during spotlighting trips over the past few years.

The "rediscovery" of the fluffy glider on the tablelands prompted the decision to present some of my observations on possums in this book, although I would not have contemplated it if Kay had not agreed to give so much of her time and care to the illustrations.

Dr John Winter, a zoologist with the Queensland National Parks and Wildlife Service, was a most generous teacher and companion from the very beginning, when he pointed out the first rainforest possum I had ever seen. Our friendship continues despite the considerable effort which the discussion and correction of my manuscript has required.

Interesting and valuable information, generously given, by David Fleay, Kevin Sparks, Rob Atherton, Margaret Winter, Dick Allison and Bernie Hyland are gratefully acknowledged. I am indebted to Dr Michael Archer of the University of New South Wales for the information on the lengths of the various possums described in this book (see Appendix A).

Jim Dawson spurred me to the search for fluffy gliders. Frank Wieland provided the clue which led to finding a colony of these animals for which David Cassells of the Queensland Forestry Department has secured protection.

My mother-in-law, Yvonne Dymock has befriended this project throughout. In addition to typing the manuscript she provided an excellent picture of a juvenile Herbert River ringtail possum, and processed the innumerable photographs which served as the basis for Kay's drawings.

I learnt about the soil eating habits of a common brushtail possum from observations made by Els Sloots, and would not have gone looking for squirrel gliders outside my usual range except for information provided by Ted Thomas.

My thanks to Craig Broughton, Russell Saunders and Tony Parsons who climbed to a sugar glider's den for me, laughing off the cold of a wet afternoon.

Dramatis Possumæ

Striped possum (*Dactylopsila trivirgata*)

Queensland long-tailed pigmy possum (*Cercatetus caudatus*)

Lemuroid possum (*Hemibelideus lemuroides*)

Green possum (*Pseudocheirus archeri*)

Herbert River ringtail possum (*Pseudocheirus herbertensis*)

Common ringtail possum (*Pseudocheirus peregrinus*)

Common brushtail possum (*Trichosurus vulpecula*)

Coppery brushtail possum (*Trichosurus vulpecula johnstonii*)

Greater glider (*Schoinobates volans*)

Feathertail glider (*Acrobates pygmaeus*)

Sugar glider (*Petaurus breviceps*)

Squirrel glider (*Petaurus norfolcensis*)

Fluffy glider (*Petaurus australis*)

Possums of
the Rainforest

Striped Possum

The track we walked on divided the rainforest around us. Our lights probed the forest, pitch dark on an overcast night. Kay and I were "spotlighting" to locate and watch possums.

We paused to listen to a pattering sound which came from a short way off in the forest. I thought there might be a group of fruit-bats feeding in the canopy, shedding fragments of their meal. Moving in amongst the trees to pick up a sample of whatever was falling, I found it was not bits of fruit but fragments of bark which were showering down.

The chips of bark were dropping from a massive, leaning tree which towered above the undergrowth. Staring up through the gaps in the shrub foliage, I caught sight of an animal, head down on the trunk. It was stabbing its lower incisor teeth into the bark of the tree, lifting out a sizeable piece with each jerk of its head. The striking white "V" marking on its forehead and the black stripes running the whole length of the body identified the animal as a striped possum.

Absorbed in the hunt for insect larvae concealed beneath the bark, the possum clung to the tree with widespread feet, while jerking out more, and still more of the bark. At times it clawed away a loosened chip with a quick movement. Through binoculars I could make out the very long fourth toe on each front foot, with which the striped possum is said to delve into borer tunnels for the beetle larvae which form part of its diet.

The possum did not seem to be the least concerned at my presence, so I went back to the track and guided Kay to the spot. Our combined noise and even our conversation caused no interruption to the possum's hunting, which was bringing it slowly down the trunk. Its long tail arched forward at times so that the

A striped possum absorbed in the hunt for insect larvae.

white tip waved above the possum's head. If there were any insects beneath the bark they must have been very small and quickly snapped up, for we could see no pauses while the possum delved or chewed. We watched until our necks ached.

Having seen a striped possum at work on the bark of a tree, I flinched in anticipation of the time when I might catch and handle one. The most memorable capture occurred on a night when I was guiding two friends on a possum-watching excursion. A rustling in the foliage led to the sighting of a striped possum about eight metres up in a tree. We gazed in delight until the possum began to fidget a little, at which I switched off the spotlight and waited until it had relaxed. When I could hear no more movement, I switched on the light and found the possum again, sitting in another tree. While it watched us calmly, I began to assess my chances of catching it. An Australian Broadcasting Commission-Television camera crew was arriving in a few days time to compile a film on rainforest animals and, as there could be no better gift to greet them with than a striped possum, I decided to make an attempt.

Warning my friends that my effort would almost certainly be in vain, I asked them to humour me by illuminating the quarry while I climbed. It so happened that a stout liane led straight up to a major limb of the tree, well above where the possum was sitting. I scaled this vine and then climbed down to the main fork of the tree. The possum scampered away along the limb it had been on, and luckily took the right fork, which did not connect with any other tree. I edged out until I had command of the decisive fork, and then shook the limb gently. The possum raced towards me, hoping to rush by to the safety of the other fork, but I grabbed its tail. It let out a menacing yell, but clung to the branch rather than turning to attack my hand. In a moment I had a bag over my prize and slid down the tree, gleeful, but gagged by the bag, a corner of which I held between my teeth. The striped possum filled the bag and the surrounding atmosphere with a very strong, repellent scent, for which, under the circumstances, I forgave it. We turned for home greatly elated, although I was already anticipating the problems of housing and feeding my captive.

The striped possum, a male, was placed in a wire cage which I crammed with an assortment of food, so that it could not turn in any direction without finding some. I put in bananas, because there are records of striped possums raiding banana plantations, and peanut butter, which is attractive to so many animals; grasshoppers from the garden to tempt its insectivorous tastes, and a small cup of honey. In the morning I was utterly dismayed to find that the poor animal had smeared its tail and hindquarters heavily with honey and had spread a little over most of the rest of its body. Blaming myself for having exposed it to this uncomfortable situation, I knew there was no alternative than to give it a bath. Kay filled a tub with warm water and, restraining the possum as firmly as possible, I immersed it, all except its head, while Kay sponged repeatedly until it was thoroughly clean. Fortunately its face needed only a little swabbing.

Next I wrapped it in a towel which I worked against its fur. The possum seemed relaxed now, so even after it was thoroughly dry I sat cuddling it to warm its body and, without doubt, for the unique pleasure of cuddling a striped possum. Throughout the bathing it had bitten only once with full savagery. Its lower incisors, over 1.5 cm long, had penetrated my thumb as easily as though they were surgical scalpels, but the upper incisors had only bruised the skin. This was because the upper incisors in this species are broad and blunt, as though worn down. I cannot think of any advantage to the possum, but was grateful that the bite was only half as bad as it could have been.

The striped possum had fed only on the banana which had been provided, so I decided to look for grubs in the rainforest. Fallen logs often show the marks of a striped possum's hunting, deep gouges where it has chewed into the timber to secure an insect. Now I began breaking open rotten logs and had soon collected a variety of pale bodied insect-larvae. Larvae such as these, together with more bananas, constituted the possum's diet for the remainder of its period in captivity.

During all the prompting and posing it was subjected to in the next few days, the striped possum never gave me a serious bite, although it frequently administered a cautionary nibble. Each time this happened I felt a rush of affection towards it, knowing just how punishing it could be in a different mood. Late one afternoon, after it had been adequately filmed, I took it back to the tree off which it had been captured. It bounded up the trunk for the first few metres, then paused and looked down at me. I could almost hear it saying, "Now what was all that about?" Unable to explain, I gave it my best wishes and withdrew.

Striped possums appear to have very large feet; this impression is perhaps emphasized by the fact that the white fur covering them is very short. All the toes on the front feet, particularly the fourth toe, are long and almost hairless. An unexplained feature on the front feet is a sort of tubercle jutting backwards from the wrist. A similar outgrowth, but so small that it is barely discernible, can also be seen on the hind feet. This lightly built possum can run very fast on the ground, which suggests that it may spend quite a lot of time in travelling or hunting at ground level, possibly in the course of investigating fallen logs. Even so, each leg is swung outward through a slightly horizontal arc at every pace, so that the gait resembles that of a lizard. It is said to "sound" for borer tunnels by tapping the limb it is hunting over (Breeden, 1970). Though I have not seen this, I have watched one slapping the pad of the front foot lightly and very rapidly in a patting motion against the wood of a dead tree it was moving over.

Quick and alert, striped possums are too seldom seen to permit estimates on the density of their population in a given area. They are not restricted to rainforest habitats, for both Frank Little, the fine naturalist of Mount Molloy, and I have seen them in eucalypt-dominated open forest. Frank once collected two female striped possums, one of which was carrying a pouch joey, from a den in the hollow limb of a bloodwood tree. The females intimated their presence by having a daytime squabble just as Frank was passing beneath their home tree. In a walk through the area, he pointed out that there were many big acacias (*Acacia aulacocarpa*) about, beneath which he often saw shreds of bark and wood chewed out by striped possums hunting for borer grubs.

The striped possum I saw in open forest appeared as if by magic one June morning. This was in a patch of forest where I had spent more than thirty-five spotlighting hours over a five-month period and had never before seen, nor expected to see a striped possum. On a pre-dawn visit, I sighted a long-tailed animal staring at me from a low branch some distance off. Unsure of its identity, I went closer, at which it turned side-on to me and climber higher into the tree. The distinctive stripes of the animal confirmed that here, in forest I had thought myself familiar with, was a totally unexpected animal.

It seemed that I had inadvertently obstructed the possum's route to its den and now, disturbed by my presence and the bright spotlight, its behaviour was agitated. It ran haphazardly about amongst the branches of the tree, often leaping down, or across between one limb and another. Finally, it ran down the tree, through the coarse blady grass and up another tall sapling. From here it stared repeatedly in the direction of a large tree which stood about ten metres away. I had by now moved around so that I was following the possum rather than heading it off. I stayed well back, watching anxiously, for it seemed that the possum was planning to jump rather than to run down and across the ground as it had done previously. After a minute or two of hesitation the striped possum leapt out, but of course, crashed heavily to the grass, falling from a height of at least thirteen metres.

There was no sound of movement for a few seconds, but then the possum ran, a little wobbly at first, and climbed the tree it had been intent upon. Having reached this tree, it covered a distance of about one hundred metres without ever descending to the ground, leaping every gap it encountered, sometimes covering four metres in a single leap. On occasions when it landed in foliage which rustled loudly at the impact, the striped possum immediately let out a short burst of its menacing threat call, as though to announce its identity to any other animal occupying the tree it had gained.

Following its progress, I saw it enter a hollow limb close to the top of a stringybark tree, perhaps thirty metres above ground. I saw a striped possum on three of my next four visits to the area, presumably the same animal, as active as ever. I never saw it actually eating anything, but as the sightings were spaced out over the following month, it could be assumed that the possum was finding an adequate diet in the open bushland, many kilometres from the nearest rainforest.

Queensland Long-tailed Pigmy Possum

New Guinea is inhabited by our species of striped possum, together with similar animals in the genera *Dactylopsila* and *Dactylonax*. Zoologists assume that the striped possum arrived in Australia via a land bridge which once existed between the two countries. Our two species of cuscus and the recently discovered soft-haired tree mouse (*Pogonomys* sp.) also originate in New Guinea and have migrated by the same route. A few Australian animals moved across in the opposite direction and are extant in New Guinea. The agile wallaby (*Macropus agilis*), for instance, and one of our pigmy possums, the Queensland long-tailed pigmy possum, occurs there.

As far as I know, I was the first person in Queensland to succeed in trapping one of these possums alive, when I once set a few box traps on the branches of rainforest trees. Having checked the traps on each of four consecutive mornings without recording anything of particular interest, I was taking down the traps on the fifth morning. It was an onerous chore, made worse by a depressing drizzle, but my complaints were forgotten when I climbed to the last trap.

In it, a little damp from the drizzle, was an animal I had never seen before. Its most noticeable features were a narrow, pointed muzzle, big dark eyes and a long thin tail. We stared at each other through the mesh of the trap. I was completely ignorant of its identity until I thought of looking at its hind feet. The first toe of each hind foot was short, clawless and rather bulbously expanded at the tip. It was set a little apart from the other toes and was clearly opposable to them, as could be seen when the animal gripped the mesh floor of its cage. The next two toes were united except that the claws were free, though closely paired. This was the typical possum hind foot, so the little animal, smaller than a rat, was clearly a species of possum.

I covered the trap with my shirt to give the occupant some protection from the drizzle and rushed home full of excitement. I riffled through a couple of reference books before telephoning John Winter. Cautiously I suggested that I had caught a Queensland long-tailed pigmy possum and John threatened he'd refuse to believe me were the animal to escape before he arrived to see it. A few hours later he confirmed its identity and he and Margaret took it into their keeping. The tiny possum flourished for many months on a special high protein and carbohydrate diet supplied by Margaret which was supplemented by grapes, apples, moths and grasshoppers. Subsequently, Rob Atherton, John's technical assistant, has trapped several more of these pigmy possums, and the National Parks and Wildlife Service now have the nucleus of a breeding colony.

Long-tailed pigmy possums are thought to live in small colonies, and their young — up to four at a time have been

This tiny animal was identified as the long-tailed pigmy possum, possibly the first to be trapped alive in Queensland.

recorded — are left in the nest when a mother finds them too large to carry about in her pouch.[1] An unusual feature in the metabolism of this species is that the adult sinks into a state of torpor on cold days. To see a pigmy possum in this condition makes one think it is on the point of death. It lies on its side with its hands and feet clenched on its abdomen. Its ears are limp and the lips are drawn back from the teeth as though due to dessication. It takes quite a lot to rouse it from this state, yet, left to itself, it becomes as active as ever after dark. Torpor is known to occur in several small mammals, but usually this energy-conserving technique is a response to a harsh climate, whether hot or cold, harsher by far than that of the tropical rainforests.

Based on studies of the fossil record, zoologists guess that the progenitor of the possum family was a small marsupial insectivore, which may not have been very different to our present day pigmy possums, the smallest of which is only about fifteen centimetres long (Ride, 1970). An adult long-tailed pigmy possum is about twenty-five centimetres long, fifteen of which is tail, and weighs somewhere between twenty and thirty grams, according to age and sex. Small and spry and needing scarcely more than a leaf to conceal them from view, pigmy possums are seldom seen by spotlighters. Their very pink noses and the rather carroty base of the long thin tail are useful field guides. The tail is often curled up quite tightly, but the result is not a neat coil, for the individual bones in the tail are quite long, and so scantily fleshed that one can see a change in angle at the beginning of every new segment. The tail is efficiently prehensile, and the little animal can readily climb its own tail should it hang down from a support by the tail alone. The long-tailed pigmy possum also uses its tail as a guy rope when standing up on its hind legs to examine something overhead.

The only sound I have ever heard from a long-tailed pigmy possum is a minute throaty roar delivered with the jaws agape. This sound, in response to a threat when they are cornered, is very similar to that given by a sminthopsis (*Sminthopsis larapinta*) about to be picked up.

In 1976, John and I made a discovery which should provide plentiful sightings of long-tailed pigmy possums, at least during the flowering period of a particular species of tree. The tree, bumpy satinash (*Eugenia cormiflora*), is quite plentiful and widely distributed; it bears its nectar-yielding flowers on the trunk, almost down to ground level. I had noticed that the nectar of these flowers was attractive to honeyeaters during the day, so we took special notice of them one night and were rewarded with the sight of a pigmy possum engrossed with the flowers. Before long another two arrived to share in the feast, and one could stand quite close by to watch without their taking fright. We went off to check on three or four similar trees I knew of, and found at least one pigmy possum in attendance at each tree.

Lemuroid Possum

One intensive period of possum-watching I was involved with began in the summer of 1976, when there was a proposal by the Australian Broadcasting Commission to make a film of rainforest animals. The first requirement was to find a densely populated area in which camera and floodlighting equipment could be concentrated. News of the project had come through John, who was engaged in a survey of various localities to suit the purpose. I volunteered to search for a suitable area in Herberton Range, as I knew it to be well populated by possums, and it was close to home. I began by walking fairly quickly along a track in the rainforest, starting just after dark, and mentally recording the numbers of various species seen. At the same time I memorized each tree on which I saw a possum, on the assumption that, so early in the evening, it would not be far from its home tree. After several such walks, I decided on a particular section of the Range, traversed by about sixty metres of track, as being sufficiently well populated. At this stage I invited John to have a look at the area; he agreed that it would suit the purpose of the film makers and would also be a good site in which we could do some consistent possum-watching. We christened this site the "Study Area".

The next step was to arrive well before dark and settle down to await nightfall, watching one of the trees in which a possum had been previously seen. This work was divided between as many possum-watchers as could come along. It was Margaret Winter who located the first den when she saw a lemuroid ringtail possum appear from a hole in the trunk of a big tree.

The lemuroid possum is named for its resemblance to one of the Madagascascar primates. It has the prettiest face of all the

Pigmy possums attracted to nectar-yielding flowers.

ringtails, with round eyes set in a fairly distinct forehead, and a small, pointed muzzle. Its eyes reflect a spotlight brilliantly, so that one can catch sight of it even when it is aloft in the crown of some giant emergent tree. I think of the lemuroid as the high climber amongst rainforest possums, for, although it does feed and rest as low as four metres from the ground, it is much more often seen in the high canopy. The lemuroid is a sure and willing jumper. It can cover a distance of about one metre in an upward bound, but its most spectacular leaps occur when jumping downward from a higher to a lower part of the canopy, causing a surprisingly loud crash for so small an animal. When jumping, it spreads its limbs widely, as though it were a glider. Another similarity to the gliders is that the lemuroid has a long tail which is fully furred with long hair, except for the tip, which is naked and much like a diminutive human finger.

I doubt that this dark brown, soft furred animal will ever find it useful to evolve a full gliding membrane, for, sooner or later, it would probably get irretrievably snagged in lawyer palm. I feel that the small ears, almost concealed by the fur of the head, are an evolutionary response by this possum, and the other two rainforest ringtails, to the thick and sometimes spiny foliage they move amongst.

Lemuroid possums are more often seen in pairs than singly. The two animals are seldom separated by more than a few metres, and usually follow the same route through the canopy. Sometimes one sees an obvious size difference between a pair of lemuroid possums, so that the animals can be judged to be a mother accompanied by a well grown joey. At most times, though, neither animal is clearly larger than its companion. Whether a mated pair keeps company for many months of the year or whether a joey follows its mother even after it appears to be fully grown, is not known. There is one record of an adult male and female found in an elkhorn clump growing on a tree felled by foresters. The female carried a pouch joey, but even in this case the male might have been her yearling offspring. I have seen three lemuroid possums together quite often, and have twice seen four in the same tree, so that this species might be considered the most sociable of the rainforest inhabiting ringtail possums. John Winter mentions seeing a lemuroid, separated by about fifty metres from another, coming to sit beside it when made nervous by John's presence.

The lemuroid possum has the prettiest face of all the ringtails.

The lemuroid is a high climber amongst rainforest possums.

I once caught a very young lemuroid possum which used two kinds of distress calls. One is a wheezing squeal, and the other is a throaty exhalation similar to that heard from so many marsupials in distress. I have heard it from joey kangaroos, marsupial mice and several species of possum. The adult lemuroid can utter a loud, long and ghastly scream, though the possum uttering it appears quite nonchalant. I can best describe the noise as similar to the sound of air escaping from a balloon while a person constricts the aperture, even to the last "phurrr" as all the air is released.

When first captured, these possums, male or female, can, and usually do, emit a penetrating musky smell which is probably designed as a repellent. It has not proved strong enough to deter me from handling them, nor did it benefit one lemuroid which we saw disappearing inside a carpet python. The snake was about three metres up a sarsaparilla tree, where it had presumably struck at a passing lemuroid. Only the hind feet and the very distinctive tail were still in view when we happened to see the glistening body of the successful hunter engulfing the last of its meal. Chance plays such a large part in the success of a python's hunting that I usually take the part of the snake when I see one with a nicely rounded bulge tucked within its midriff.

At rest during the night, lemuroid possums sit in a hunched ball with the tail pushed forward a little, the distal half coiled quite tightly, but not around any anchorage. This observation was not made until John and I took to using spotlights masked with red cellophane. Using a similarly masked spotlight for pre-dawn visits I have followed pairs of lemuroids until both animals have entered a common den.

Herbert River Ringtail Possum

One night when Kay and I were spotlighting in the rainforest of Herberton Range, we saw a very small possum sitting amongst dense undergrowth foliage. I could not tell whether it was a baby animal or a species of small possum which had never been previously recorded. In either case, the colour of its fur, a very pale caramel shade, matched only one possum I knew of, the *cinereus* sub-species of the Herbert River ringtail possum. This pale coloured sub-species has been recorded in the vicinity of Mt

Lewis, further north, and a positive identification of a juvenile *cinereus* from Herberton Range would be of considerable interest.

While Kay used the spotlight to keep track of the tiny possum I clambered amongst the undergrowth and heaved energetically on the entangling vines until at last the little animal fell with a plop into a pile of leaf litter. We found that its appearance matched that of *cinereus* very closely; not only was its fur the right colour, but it also showed the cinnamon brown streak running down the centre of its forehead, a characteristic feature of the northern sub-species.

We took it home and housed it in a roomy cage. I presented a wide variety of fruit to our little captive, from which it selected a pear on its first night with us. When John Winter came over to look at it he confidently pronounced it to be a juvenile Herbert River ringtail of the standard species, but agreed that it did look much like a *cinereus*. He had no objections to our rearing the youngster, partly in order to watch its development, and also to discover what food it would accept in captivity before transferring it to the National Parks and Wildlife Service establishment in Pallarenda.

The baby, a female, was named Yvonne. After two and a half months she lost her *cinereus* colouring and grew much darker, with a very glossy coat. Always defiant and threatening, she greeted any intrusion into her cage with explosive screeches even though I came carrying fresh supplies of food. I learned that she was very fond of eating flowers. Crepe-myrtle, bottlebrush, roses, nasturtium, cannas and quisqualis were amongst her favourites. She liked the young leaves of mistletoe, bottlebrush, mango, weeping fig and both young and mature leaves of the broad-leafed peppercorn (*Schinus terebinthifolia*). Amongst fruits she usually chose bananas and tomatoes, refusing paw-paw, apples and oranges, although I have known other Herbert River ringtails to accept these readily.

Nearly five months after her capture she went down to Townsville with John, and is still doing well more than a year later.

Since our first meeting with Yvonne I have seen many juvenile Herbert River possums, many of which look quite as much like *cinereus* as she did, although some are darker from the outset and others, on close examination, can be seen to have pale, nearly white stripes across the upper arm and sometimes across the thigh

Yvonne was the name given to this young Herbert River ringtail.

as well. September to November are the months when most baby Herbert River possums are to be seen, usually sitting solemnly in the undergrowth. It seems that the female Herbert River possum, which usually rears two offspring at a time, evades her joeys when they are much younger, than does any other species of possum. One mother we watched in the "Study Area" was bulging with two big pouch joeys when first seen. Within two weeks of that sighting the joeys were "at heel", although they still clung to her in tense moments, and a week later one of the joeys was seen in a thicket without any sign of the mother nearby.

One night in November of 1978 two Herbert River ringtails were seen in open forest at the site inhabited by the Forest Colony fluffy gliders. One of these animals was sighted on several subsequent occasions, and was seen to eat eucalyptus (*E. intermedia*)leaves, and mistletoe. In mid-April 1979 this animal was seen to enter a drey, carrying two young on her back. The drey was built in a mistletoe clump growing on a turpentine (*Syncarpia gomulifera*) tree, and the young were observed to continue sharing the drey with their mother for the next twelve days, even though the mother left alone each night, and the joeys, on emerging about ten minutes later, moved about independently, with no attempt to follow their mother. These observations on Herbert River ringtails provide a unique record of this species utilizing an open forest habitat.

The typical colour pattern of adult Herbert River possums is black above and white below, with an all-black head, and the distal half of the tail white. At the same time there is wide variation in the colouring of this species, both as regards the intensity of the dark parts, which may be dark brown, grey or jet, and the amount of white fur distributed over the body. Some may have only the tail tip white in an otherwise uniformly dark body. Others have a white chest patch, white throat and chest, or are white over the entire underside. A further elaboration of the pattern is the presence of a white band across the upper arms in some specimens and, more rarely, a similar stripe across the thighs. Stephen van Dyck of the Queensland Museum has collected one which was white throughout, except for a dark head and an elongate black patch over the lower back.

From our observations in the "Study Area" we found that some Herbert River possums used hollows in tree trunks for their dens,

The striking black and white pattern of this Herbert River possum is common for this species.

while others emerged from large clumps of elkhorn or mistletoe growing in the canopy. To judge from rudimentary nest building by the captive, Yvonne, it is probable that this species collects nesting material to cushion its rump. Even though they have short rough fur, it wears thin on their rumps upon which they are accustomed to sit while asleep.

The first concern of a Herbert River possum, after emerging from its den, seems to be a thorough grooming session. It scratches with the grooming claws, removes anything caught in them with its teeth, and then scratches again. Between times it tugs vigorously at the fur of its chest and shoulders with its teeth, so vigorously that one expects to see mouthfuls of fur spat out. Grooming completed, the possum moves either up or down in the forest, either climbing higher to feed on leaves, blossoms or fruits, or coming down to within two metres of the ground to eat leaves of the understorey growth. This species is the only rainforest possum we have seen eating mistletoe, and it may in fact eat quite a lot of epiphytic growth, for it is often seen on the major limbs of a tree.

It is not uncommon to hear the staccato growling of a Herbert River possum during some treetop altercation; this is the only vocalization known to me. Aggressive behaviour towards a human captor includes rearing up on the hindlegs to claw with the front feet, while making growling and spitting protests. This posturing is mostly bluff put on to deter the enemy. Only once have I known a Herbert River possum to worry the flesh it had hold of: my flesh. This was more like the thoroughgoing performance given by a cuscus; most possum bites are just quick snaps which are not very painful.

Green Possum

A small animal was crossing the highway after dark. Used to seeing rufous rat-kangaroos and bandicoots crossing the road, I casually steered our car around it. Then, out of the corner of my eye, I saw it had a short fat tail. Wheeling the car around to illuminate the scene, I ran back just in time to see my quarry climbing a bank covered in elephant grass. It tried to ascend one of these grass stems, which of course bent down under its weight and deposited a green possum on my head. Clutching its fat tail, I ran back to the car with the possum still clinging to my scalp.

I popped it into a pillow case, knowing that John Winter would be happy to take it into captivity, for at that stage he was planning a series of animal houses in which possums could be kept and studied. During the time that the green possum lived in John's home in Atherton, a number of people sought introduction to her. I heard that at least one of them, before seeing a green possum for the first time, had scoffed unbelievingly when Margaret mentioned it.

The classical green possum has a decidedly lime green coat, grizzled with white and yellow. There is a dark vertebral stripe bordered by two silvery white stripes, these again edged with darker fur. The whole pattern is not sharply defined but rather diffused, and seems to slip and twist over its back when a green possum is on the move. The face is quite intricately marked, with snow white patches above and below the eye and at the base of the ear. The short muzzle is tipped with a pink nose. The green hue of the fur is known to take its colour from a combination of black, white and yellow pigments (Ride, 1970). This probably explains why the colour of some individuals inclines towards grey or yellow.

A green possum's coat feels dense and resilient to the touch, but if roughly handled the lovely fur will pull out in tufts. It is not uncommon to see a wisp or even a tiny pile of its fur adrift in the forest, but whether this easily shed fur is of any help in evading the grasp of an owl or python I do not know. When a green possum is accompanied by a large back-riding joey her rump often looks quite tattered owing to the fur lost because of her clutching infant.

We used to stand and marvel at the green possum which John kept when it was absorbed in a grooming session. There is one stage in the proceedings which is quite astonishing. In order to attend to the fur in the middle of its back, it swings around to spread the fur with both hands so that the teeth and tongue can get to work. The reversal of the upper half of the body is so complete that it really looks as though the possum has been taken apart midway and reassembled with the top half facing the wrong way round.

Baby green possums, just out of the pouch, are possibly the prettiest of all joeys, for at this stage their fur is still short and

The green possum has silvery stripes running the length of its back.

pressed close to the body in a slightly waved and very brightly coloured coat. I have never seen a mother accompanied by more than one young, though theoretically two babies could be raised simultaneously, as the pouch is furnished with two teats. At one time Rob Atherton, together with two other observers, recorded a green possum accompanied by three joeys, all clinging to her back. This astonishing feat by the mother suggests that she had accepted at least one, if not two foster babies, unless she had given birth to all three of them, and had three teats in her pouch, which does occur very rarely.[2] How she managed is hard to imagine, for a mother carrying just one joey on her back is obviously labouring at times when she has to push her way through a tangle of branches or climb up a vine. Quite often the baby is forced off by thick foliage and has to catch up as best it can. I have never heard a lagging baby call out, and in fact the green possum may be the most silent of the large possums, for I have never heard one call, not even at the moment of capture.

The green possum may breed in most months of the year for we have seen joeys riding on their mother's backs in early February, mid-June and mid-November.

Green possums have been seen asleep in thickets or even in fairly open trees in the daytime, presumably trusting to their cryptic colours. The only other Australian *Phalangerid* I know of which sleeps out is the spotted cuscus, and it, again like the green possum, has been seen feeding during the day in dull weather. Independence from particular den trees may enable the green possum to exploit a forest more widely and it would be interesting to establish if this possum is less bound to a particular feeding range than other possum species.

I feel that the green possum is better fitted to survive than either the lemuroid or the Herbert River possum where a rainforest habitat is severely disturbed by heavy logging, or reduced to a mere "island" due to destruction of the surrounding forest. Its ability to rest in thickets frees it from dependence on dens which are generally only available in well grown trees. Dietary factors may also contribute to its survival under marginal conditions. For instance, it is known to eat the leaves of various fig trees, and these trees are not harvested in logging operations. Two unexpected items in its diet which we have recorded are the leaves of the mulberry-leafed stinging tree (*Dendrocnide photinphylla*)

A sleeping green possum curled into a furry ball.

and glycine. Glycine is a pasture legume which often overruns the shrubs growing on the edges of rainforest adjacent to pasturelands.

The relatively insecure daytime roosts used by the green possum may account for its sleepiness early in the night. It sleeps or rests in a very characteristic posture, curled into a furry green ball, possibly as early as 8 P.M. for the first nap of the night. Unless a masked spotlight is used, the possum often uncurls and moves off due to intruders. I once saw a green possum uncurl and as she rose a joey uncurled from within her folds. As the mother walked away the baby climbed onto her rump, the whole proceeding performed smoothly, as though choreographed. Still larger joeys curl up beside their mothers, nose to nose or side by side.

Coppery Brushtail Possum

Late one night I drove to the Crater National Park intending to spotlight along the path which runs through the forest. On returning to the carpark I passed a big open-topped drum used as a litter bin. There was a loud crash. Jerking on the switch of the spotlight I swung around, expecting to see an assailant emerge from behind the drum. A large reddish possum leapt from the bin and scuttled off.

The coppery brushtail possum tends to scavenge in park areas and may even become bold enough to accept scraps thrown by visitors. It can run fast on the ground and it is this ability which emboldens it to hunt around picnic tables and scamper between people's feet after dark.

This animal (*Trichosurus vulpecula johnstonii*) is a sub-species of the common brushtail possum (*Trichosurus vulpecula*) which is widespread in open forests of eastern Australia. Brushtail possums are classified in the family *Phalangeridae* which also includes the cuscuses and the scaly-tailed possum. The green, lemuroid and Herbert River possums are members of the ringtail possum group, in the family *Petauridae*. The coppery brushtail is easily distinguished from the other possums living in the rainforest as it has prominent pointed ears and a short dark tail. A well coloured specimen has a reddish brown coat, although paler yellowish brown and even grey individuals may be seen.

A variety of growls, grunts and squeals are part of the coppery brushtail's repertoire.

This species of possum frequently eats the foliage of a particular shrub, the wild tobacco (*Solanum mauritianum*), which none of the rainforest ringtails have been seen eating. This is a pioneer plant in disturbed rainforest, often growing densely beside forest tracks. It is known that the leaves of wild tobacco contain very toxic alkaloids (Van Dyck, 1978), yet the coppery brushtail and other members of its genus, *Trichosurus*, are able to eat them without coming to any harm. It is the only species I have seen feeding on acacias growing on the verges of rainforest, and is the possum most often seen in the bleeding heart tree (*Omolanthus populifolius*).

Quite frequently, just after passing a coppery brushtail sitting in a tree, it lets out a strange call which used to make my hair bristle until I came to expect it. This call is a sort of grating, stuttering growl, which John Winter describes as a "brief chatter" (Winter, 1976). He says that it is uttered in response to a mildly stressful situation, in this case, the disturbance occasioned by the spotlighter. Sometimes a prolonged commotion in the forest is heard which sounds like the noises made by quarrelling pigs, so varied are the growls, grunts and squeals, but all these vocalizations coming from up in the trees are part of the coppery brushtail's repertoire.

Successful spotlighting in rainforest is restricted almost entirely to areas traversed by vehicle tracks. In general, a spotlighter is obliged to keep to tracks because this offers the opportunity to view a vertical profile of the forest. The chief difficulty in looking up from within the forest itself is that the lowermost foliage reflects the spotlight beam so strongly that animals higher up are screened by the glare. Besides, the trees are taller and their first branches much further from the ground, so that even the animals seen at the expense of an aching neck, are usually far up and consequently difficult to watch.

By keeping to a track special precautions do not have to be taken against getting lost. It also enables quieter movement. In the hundreds of hours which I have occupied with spotlighting, only two snakes have been encountered across my path and neither of them could be regarded as dangerously venomous. One was a small-eyed snake (*Cryptophis nigrescens*) and the other a brown tree snake (*Boiga irregularis*). Probably the slow progress involved in spotlighting allows snakes ample time to move out of the way.

Most vehicular tracks in rainforests imply a disturbance of the original vegetation, so that many of the wayside trees are "regeneration species", tolerant of bared soil, increased sunlight and a higher wind intensity. The swathe cut by a track also permits a dense growth of shrubs and vines. These conditions do not appear to diminish the possum population. More possums are seen, both in numbers and variety of species, in regeneration areas than within adjacent climax forest.

Secondary species of trees found growing beside a track are smaller and can be scanned more easily and this may have a lot to do with the fact that more possums are seen in disturbed forests. Another factor may be that rainforest possums have a dietary preference for some of those trees and shrubs characteristic of regeneration growth. Regrowth species extensively eaten by possums include sarsaparilla (*Alphitonia petrei, A. whiteii*), candlenut (*Aleurites moluccana*) and celery top (*Panax murrayi*). Leaves of the bleeding heart tree (*Omolanthus populifolius*) are also eaten occasionally, while amongst shrubs one which is very popular belongs to the *Rhodamnia* genus.

Amongst climax species known to be eaten by rainforest possums are the northern silky oak (*Cardwellia sublimis*), the silver quondong (*Elaeocarpus grandis*), sassafras (*Doryphora aromatica*), white carbeen (*Sloanea langii*) and maple (*Flindersia brayleana*).

Selective logging as practised in northern state forests does not seem likely to endanger the endemic possum population, but one requirement which should be deliberately provided for is the retention of a sufficient number of large old trees which provide adequate den sites. If a good number of such trees are preserved, even though they might not be commercially valuable species, the possum population would receive considerable benefit. The "Study Area" for instance, is situated in a heavily disturbed site, but within it there are a number of big trees, some dead (ringbarked) and others still alive, presumably unharvested because they have faulty boles. The numerous dens provided by these trees may account, in part, for the high population recorded in this area: along a sixty metre stretch of track through this patch of rainforest we sometimes saw as many as twelve possums of four different species, in the space of an hour.

There are more eyes in the night than those of possums. Frogs' eyes shine brightly, and a tree frog high up in the canopy can present a puzzle. Its eyes, set fairly widely apart, are suggestive of an animal the size of a big rat, but unless one uses binoculars, the small body of the frog can scarcely be seen. Leaf-tailed geckos usually station themselves on a tree trunk, head down, watching for insects on the move below them. Their flattened, camouflaged bodies are hard to make out, and if one is using a bright spotlight they usually contract their pupils soon after the light strikes them, so that the animals seem to vanish. Snakes' eyes are not generally reflective though I have once picked up very dull eyeshine from the eyes of a carpet python, but only from a certain angle. On the track one may see various frogs and cane toads, and sometimes a dingo or feral cat pads along, unaware of its human observer. Bandicoots and pademelons are not rare but they usually hop off rather promptly. Water rats are sometimes seen foraging along the track and *Melomys* and giant white-tailed rats may be seen in the trees.

The biggest mammal one is likely to come across in the trees is Lumholtz's tree kangaroo on the tablelands. Too often it leaps down from the trees and crashes its way through the forest before one has seen it, but at times it stays put, staring at the spotlighter, seemingly determined to do nothing interesting until after the intruder has moved away. It has very dull, ruby red eyeshine, and seldom gives itself away by slight movements, both factors contributing to the relatively rare occasions on which one sees this interesting animal.

Owls' eyes reflect a spotlight quite strongly; the three species most commonly seen in tableland rainforests are the little boobook, the handsome sooty owl and the big rufous owl. On the homeward leg of a spotlighting trip with Ralph and Daffi Keller, nature photographers from Melbourne, someone saw a pair of widely spaced eyes belonging to a largish animal sitting in a sarsaparilla tree. All of us were tired and began to guess at its identity instead of looking carefully. I assumed it was a coppery brushtail possum; Ralph suggested it was a tree kangaroo, but then where was its tail, and why was it so dangerously far out on a brittle limb. By now we were almost beneath it and discovered to our shame that it was a rufous owl, which flew from its perch as we chaffed each other. As it flew we saw a small insectivorous bat pursuing it, diving down onto its back just as a mobbing bird would do. Whether daytime roosts of small bats are ever raided by

Green possums are sometimes seen abroad in daylight.

owls I do not know, but this owl was plainly being treated as an enemy by the tiny bat.

More magical than one's own spotlight are the tiny lights which shine in the rainforest. Flitting through the trees in the warm months can be seen scores of fireflies. In tiny caves in damp earthen banks beside the track there may be blue-glowing *arachnocampa* larva, waiting to collect the insects trapped by the sticky-beaded curtain it hangs across the entrance to its retreat. On a warm and humid night there may be hundreds of tiny, luminous fungi, little mushrooms no bigger than a match head. The mycelial threads of some fungi glow too, so that a whole dead trunk or patch of litter on the forest floor may be lit by a ghostly luminescence.

A dark, still, dry night in the rainforest is ideal for spotlighting. When the night is still, the noise of an animal moving in the foliage is more easily detected and, if it is dry, there are not thousands of glittering droplets suspended in the canopy. If there is no moon and the stars are screened out by a layer of cloud, every glint of light in the canopy is likely to be a reflection from the eyes of an animal.

A 30 watt sealed-beam spotlight operated off a 12 volt motor cycle battery provides a bright light which lasts for several hours. A "masked" spotlight is a better choice if the object is to observe the behaviour of some animals. This is a standard spotlight with a sheet of red cellophane taped over the glass, so that a red rather than a yellow light is transmitted. John Winter suggested this technique, and our experiments have shown that most of the nocturnal animals we have watched are far less perturbed than if a conventional light is used. Nowadays I use a red light almost exclusively.

The best time to commence a spotlighting trip is immediately after dark. It is best to arrive half an hour or so before dark and wait for nightfall to look for dens. In summertime the cicadas usually set up a clamour which lasts for about ten minutes, commencing a little before 7P. M. The timing of this chorus seems to be based on certain light levels, and it is at just about "cicada chorus time" that possums begin to leave their dens. Possums have rest periods later in the night, sitting about a lot between the hours of 10P. M. and 2A. M.. In the early winter they stay out until surprisingly late in the morning, well after 5A. M. for instance.

Possums of
the Open Forest

Common Brushtail Possum

Wakened by a scratching noise, I staggered out to trace the source, but whatever had disturbed my sleep was now silent, so I went back to bed. Woken again by the same noise, I discovered it came from within the flue-pipe of our little-used wood stove. I prised the flue from its junction with the stove, and succeeded in raising it about seven centimetres. In the gap was revealed the head of a brushtail possum. The animal slid still further down, to squeeze into the chamber behind the oven. Knowing it would mean a struggle to pull the possum out by the tail, I tugged the flue out of the way as far as possible and returned to bed. The possum extricated itself somehow, its departure through the window marked by a trail of gritty soot.

Of the three brushtail possums which frequently visit the eucalypts around our house, one sometimes camps on a shelf in a large, open-fronted box which stands in one corner of our yard. I went to see if it was there on the morning after the stove incident and found it fast asleep. It was crouched in a dome-shaped hump, with its neck so completely bent down that its forehead lay flat along the shelf, muzzle tucked between the front feet. Usually one cannot approach the resting possum without finding it already alerted, staring hard at the intruder, but on this occasion it slept on, undisturbed.

Kay and I have christened this possum "Steel-wool" which is not only a good description of its colour and rather coarse fur, but is also a reminder of another possum which shared our first house on the tablelands after our three years in Mount Isa. We had seen no possums in the Mount Isa area, so it was a treat to find that one lived above our ceiling. I made a small platform on the verandah, where we set out gifts of fruit and honeyed bread for the possum.

In the mornings I used to check the items we had offered to see which of them had been fancied. Red apples were preferred to green, oranges and mandarins were welcome, bananas acceptable, but honeyed bread generally finished up on the floor, sticky side down. Some nights the possum perched on the window sill, looking in at us. "Watching television", Kay said. She noticed that it would snatch up some of the moths which fluttered against the window panes. Once, the possum was out late during a prowl in our kitchen. Rather than climb back to its customary den at dawn it camped on the pantry shelves, with its back to the day. Kay mistook it for a hank of steel-wool, until she went to reach for it. Another time it strayed into baby Charlie Pickle's room and roused him by clambering over his cot. Charlie's screams brought us running in to hear a description of the intruder, in which our boy used every word and non-word of his mystifying vocabulary. Only the sound of the possum padding across the ceiling explained the commotion.

The common brushtail can settle itself in a variety of unusual retreats. It is known to use rabbit burrows on Kangaroo Island, and to roost, koala-fashion, in the forks of trees in dense New Zealand forests (Troughton, 1954). I have seen one retire to a felled hollow log and another climb from a "form" in thick grass in an area where none of the gum trees were large enough to furnish a suitable hollow limb. One of the brushtails living near our home occupies a cavity in an arboreal termitarium, the interior of which has crumbled a little since it was originally hollowed out by a pair of nesting kookaburras.

Many a suburban and rural home is tennanted by a brushtail possum which gains access to the ceiling. Herberton folk sometimes ask me to catch and remove their resident possum, but I usually beg off, for what is one to do with the animal after it is bagged? Releasing them in bushland is not a satisfactory solution for it is unlikely that they will find a feeding range and den site amongst the brushtails already resident in the area. Instead, I suggest, why not put up a box in a big tree near the house and block the possum's access after it has gone out one evening. I fear this has not led to a rash of boxes appearing in trees of the neighbourhood, but perhaps the possums are reprieved while their reluctant hosts contemplate my suggestion.

Brushtails, and indeed, all possums, eat surprisingly little in a night, but unfortunately their tastes encompass a wide variety of fruits and flowers, so that the buds one has been counting on a rose bush, or the mandarins on a backyard tree are likely to disappear prematurely. I remember throwing boots at a brushtail in a hut on Mount Feathertop. Four of us had sheltered in the hut after a tiring day's walk; we had left our packs open after a quick meal, to the delight of a possum which raided them at intervals through the night. Whenever I stirred, it retreated in the direction of the fireplace, usually carrying something away in its mouth.

The standard den used by these possums in the bush is a hollow limb in a tree. Brushtails are not sociable animals and rarely is a den shared by two adults, although I have seen a pair emerge from a very large cavity in a tree trunk. In my experience, the brushtail leaves its den earlier in the evening than any other species of possum. It can be seen sitting near its home while there is still sufficient light to distinguish the outlines of trees and shrubs, although a spotlight is needed to see the animal itself.

Large and not especially agile in trees, the brushtail usually comes down to the ground in order to cross to another tree. If not in a hurry, it ambles along with the tail held off the ground in a slight, down-curving arch. The slightest noise will cause it to stop and listen carefully, sitting erect with the front paws resting against its stomach. This lovable pose never fails to suggest to me the image of a complacent matronly figure. If the alarm is intensified, the brushtail makes a dash up the nearest tree. It can run quite fast and even jink and double back if pursued, although its speed is no match for that of a dog.

These possums eat grass, grass seeds and legumes, quite habitually when on the ground. Els Sloots, who reared an infant brushtail, pointed out that the youngster ate small quantities of earth quite often when she "walked" it after dark. It also chewed up a grasshopper presented to it, which was in keeping with the brushtail's fondness for those insects which it can catch. I have heard of them visiting the carcasses of rabbits killed on the road, but whether this was in order to eat the flesh of the animal or the vegetable matter contained in the stomach, was not clear.

Their staple diet is provided by various eucalypts, acacia and mistletoe leaves as well as mistletoe and eucalypt blossoms. Too heavy to venture safely amongst terminal foliage, a brushtail prefers to position itself on a firm branch above a choice cluster of blossoms or leaves, from where it lowers itself while clinging with the hind feet and tail.

The tail is quite short and tapering; the upper surface and sides are fur-covered, but there are neither bristles nor a tuft of hair at the tip to justify the term "brushtail". Much of the ventral surface, distally, is bare-skinned to provide the possum with a better grip on a branch. People who have kept these animals as pets are often misled into thinking their possum is a ringtail because it can coil its tail up, but the extensive, furless strip on the underside is a certain guide to identity. Although a joey can hang by its tail and turn about to reclimb it, adult brushtails grow too heavy to manage this feat.

Female brushtails rear only one joey at a time, which is usually born in the cooler months, and first leaves the pouch when about four months old. At this time its underparts are quite often a fairly bright tan or orange colour, fading to an off-white as the animal matures. The mother's pouch is not capacious enough for the baby to leap into it easily in the way a joey kangaroo does. So much awkward struggling is necessary when the baby wants to shelter in the pouch, that it soon contents itself with riding on its mother's back, only pushing its head into the pouch when sucking. Joeys remain with their mothers until about nine-months old, by which time they are following her about, "at heel". They do not seem to have much sense of fun, although the baby Els Sloots reared did at times race away from and back to her in mock alarm.

On the chest of an adult male one can see a longitudinal, rust-coloured streak which marks the location of a scent-secreting gland, present in both sexes, but more prominent in the male. In addition to this gland these possums also possess scent glands on the chin and near the cloaca. The secretions from these glands, in addition to urine and saliva deposits, are used to apply scent labels to chosen spots during a brushtail's wanderings. Information on sex, sexual receptivity of females, age and identity are thought to be transmitted by scent deposits which are used to indicate the whereabouts of a particular animal rather than the signposting of a particular territory (Winter, 1976).

Brushtails are quite vocal animals, but most of the loud noises they use towards each other are unfriendly sounds, which is in keeping with their non-gregarious natures. Their preference for solitary behaviour gives rise to mutual avoidance or a vocal and

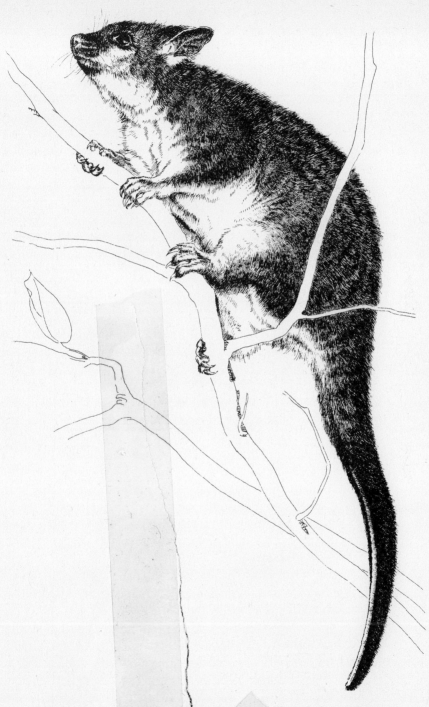

The furless strip on the underside of its tail readily distinguishes the brushtail possum from the common ringtail.

perhaps physical assault whenever a conspecific of either sex is encountered and one animal fails to give way. Tooth and claw battles are not usually very damaging, but one sometimes sees a possum which has lost the use of an eye, presumably due to an injury inflicted by the slapping claws of an opponent.

I regard them as very stolid animals, quite capable of outstaring me when I am out possum-watching. One night I sighted a brushtail feeding in an acacia before it became aware of my presence. I wanted to collect a sample of the leaves it was eating for identification, but, preferring not to frighten the possum, which was now staring at me, I went by. The possum was still in the acacia an hour later, so rather than forego the leaf sample, I approached the tree, broke off a few leaves and retired. When I was nearly out of sight, it voiced a gruff throaty comment, which it continued to repeat for many minutes afterwards.

Common Ringtail Possum

The spotlight showed a rapidly shifting constellation of six shining eyes moving through the trees. A female common ringtail possum, carrying two babies on her back, was setting out for the night's feeding. A thin branch amongst the outermost foliage of one tree bent under her weight. She dropped lightly from it and gained a hold in the crown of an adjacent tree. She hurried along, bounding across short distances at times, despite the weight of her joeys. After crossing through the tops of four trees, she walked down a stout, leaning trunk, one joey riding above her shoulders and the other clinging to her rump. Reaching the ground, the trio disappeared from sight amongst the tall bracken, through which the mother travelled for about twenty metres. I then saw her climb a broad-leafed acacia (*Acacia flavescens*) where she began to feed. One of the joeys remained on her back while the other slipped from her rump to sit beside its mother while she chewed the acacia leaves. Whenever she moved to another part of the tree, the joey regained its perch on her back.

On the following evening I was in time to see the mother ringtail climb from a den in a hollow limb, the joeys already positioned on her back. She started out along the same route as before, but then became aware of my presence and stopped to stare. Discovered, I went away, knowing the ringtail would be

The ringtail can easily climb its own tail when hanging from a branch.

prepared to wait for half an hour, or more, until satisfied that there was no danger. On three subsequent visits during the next eight days I saw the adult emerge from its den, but without her joeys. It is possible that they had grown old enough to be left in another den,[3] but if this were the case she certainly did not hurry over to them after dark, nor could I trace their eyeshine in the surrounding area. The youngsters were first observed in mid-July, and it is possible that they succumbed to a poor season or had been lost to a predator.

Earlier in the year, at the beginning of February, I saw a ringtail high in a eucalypt on two successive evenings, just after dark. Coming past the tree later on the second night, I glimpsed two joey ringtails running into a clump of twiggy branches, where they were lost to sight. I watched at that tree on the following evening; nothing stirred during the half-hour after dusk, yet later in the night a pair of eyes was glinting from the spot to which I had seen the two joeys retreat. There seemed to be a twiggy bundle wedged amongst a cluster of branches which sprouted from the site of an injury to a big limb. I climbed up the main trunk in daylight, next day, until I was level with the mass of twigs. When I poked at it gently with a long stick, a mother ringtail, carrying two joeys on her back, made a prompt exit, climbing out of the top of the nest, straight up one of the supporting branches. She sat there for a while, looking about owlishly, and then, correctly deciding that my agility in trees was minimal, returned to the nest. It was astonishing to see the ringtail and her two babies disappear so completely inside such a small nest.

This is the only ringtail nest, or "drey", I have ever seen; it seems that nest-building in the open is a rare occurrence in the north, where ringtails usually den in hollow limbs.[4] The reverse is the case in New South Wales and Victoria, where common ringtails usually build football-sized nests in dense shrubs or trees (Marsh, 1967; Thompson and Owen, 1964).

The common ringtail of the tablelands district is a pretty little animal, generally light grey on the dorsal parts, with fawn limbs and fawn markings on the face. It has large ears, the margins of which are slightly irregular in outline. The tail is long, thin and tapering, covered in short fur, grey proximally and white on the distal half. Near the tip, on the ventral surface, the fur is very sparse.

The toes on the front feet of the common ringtail are distinctively arranged, permitting a pincer grip amongst foliage.

When resting or feeding, this possum is sometimes seen sitting with its tail coiled up, and it is this habit which is alluded to in the name "ringtail", or "ring-tailed possum", applied to the common ringtail and the other members of its genus. This is, however, only an occasional habit; the tail usually hangs straight down while the possum is sitting, and is generally held out, slightly arched, when a ringtail is on the move. A common ringtail can easily hang by its tail alone and regain a foothold on the supporting branch by climbing its tail. The tip can be flexed so strongly that one has to exert considerable force to straighten it when trying to measure a captive.

The toes on the front feet of a ringtail possum are distinctively arranged. The first two toes of each foot point inwards and the next three are directed outwards. This allows a pincer grip amongst twiggy foliage, and probably provides a better hold on vertical branches than a brushtail can manage.[5] This adaptation is present in all genera of the ringtail group, excepting the less arboreal rock-haunting ringtail (*Petropseudes dahli*) (Troughton, 1954).

As with all possums, the first toe of the hind foot is clawless and bulbously expanded at the tip. It is opposable and functions as a thumb. The benefits of an efficient grip provided by the thumbs on the hind feet are best seen when a possum pauses while walking along a thin limb. From this position it can stand almost erect to reach upward, sit across a limb while reaching for food with the front feet and, most important of all, a possum can turn back to retrace its steps without needing to release the hold of its hind feet until the front paws have taken a fresh hold. Cats, rodents and other arboreal adventurers without thumbs cannot perform this manoeuvre nearly as well.

The second and third toes on the hind foot are encased within a single sheath with the claws closely adpressed. These are the "syndactyl" toes; the paired claws are referred to as the grooming claws, for they provide a useful comb when raked through the fur. The family term, *Phalangeridae*, used for possums, cuscuses and koalas, is derived from a Greek word, *phalanger*, meaning "web", a reference to the "web" encasing the second and third toes (Burton, 1969). When a ringtail is scratching with the hind foot, its leg flies up and down at a tremendous rate, after which the grooming claws are licked clean of any fur or ectoparasites wedged between them. If the back of one thigh is itchy, a possum reaches across beneath its tail with the other hind foot, to scratch with whizzing speed.

Smaller and much more agile than a brushtail possum, because it can take a better grip with the front feet and has a more efficiently prehensile tail, the ringtail possum accomplishes most of its wanderings without descending to the ground. It jumps across short distances quite habitually, pouncing neatly, without splaying its legs widely during a leap. When a narrow roadway bisects a ringail possum's feeding range, they use suitable crossover trees. Sometimes two trees arching across a roadway provide a one way crossing only, if just one limb of one tree overhangs a branch of the other. Not able to jump upwards from a flexible branch, the possum has to locate a second site where a crossing in the opposite direction can be made.

Ringtail possums are not as common in the areas I am familiar with as they are in parts of Victoria and New South Wales, where populations have been studied by zoologists (Marsh, 1967; Thompson and Owen, 1964). These possums are regarded as sociable animals, several camping together in dreys, and family groups often travelling and feeding in company. Vocal communication is said to be frequent, the sounds resembling bird-like twitterings, used by adults and well grown joeys. One observer (Marsh, 1967) reports the use of a partly ultra-sonic distress call used by two-month old joeys, presumably when manually removed from the mother's pouch. The only time I have heard a ringtail make any sound was when a female John Winter had captured gave some very loud, almost piercing squeaks.

The common ringtail feeds on a variety of leaves, fruit, nectar, bark and even seeds. While feeding amongst foliage it holds the leaves in either one or both hands, pulling them towards the mouth for each fresh mouthful. At times it pulls or bites the leaf off in order to sit back comfortably while munching. Bark from the upper surface of twigs is ripped off in short strips with the teeth, while to bite small pieces of bark from the underside of a twig, the ringtail curls downward rather like a gymnast on a horizontal bar. I have watched ringtails feeding in casurarina trees more than once, but cannot be sure whether they were eating the leaves or the male flowers.

Gliding
Possums

Greater Glider

A dense mist had settled over the forest at sunset. One might have termed it a drizzle except that the stars could be seen shining dimly through the haze, each star surrounded by a glowing halo. Big drops of water, glistening like glass beads, were falling from the leaves, often splashing against the spotlight, or into my eyes. When I held it away from me at arm's length, the light threw fascinating shadows into the mist. This was not regulation spotlighting procedure by any means, but the night was too enchanting for a disciplined walk. A brilliant flash of eyes brought my attention to the rim of a hollow, broken tree trunk from which a greater glider was peeping out. The eyes of few other possums shine so brightly that they can be seen even with indirect light.

The glider stared down at me as I approached, not deigning to retreat out of view. As I walked beneath and then past its den-tree, it leaned further and further out to watch, until finally its head was hanging upside down, still staring fixedly. When I was far enough away it climbed onto the rim of its den and from there jumped to the trunk of a tall tree. It hopped up this tree and walked out along a horizontal branch, using a high-stepping gait which held its body well off the branch. Its long tail arched stiffly, duplicating the curve of its spine. A greater glider seldom planes out of a tree if it is conscious of an intruder, so when this one stopped near the end of the branch and sat down facing me, I moved off.

Though willing to outstare a spotlighter with almost reptilian patience when outward bound, a greater glider is reluctant to be delayed when journeying back to its den in the pre-dawn hour. Successive glides can be seen at this time, despite the animal's awareness of an observer. It can cover long distances in a glide and might set a course for a tree fifty or even eighty metres away. The greater glider collects itself together carefully before taking off,

The greater glider can cover long distances in a glide.

preferring to leap from a fairly firm branch rather than the outermost foliage. Once airborne, it loses height rapidly during a long swoop, coming down to within a metre of the ground when nearing the objective. In the last seconds the glider controls its momentum by rising steeply to clutch the tree trunk it has aimed for. One can clearly hear its claws striking the bark at the moment of impact. The glider then hops rapidly up and continues its journey until safely home.

The largest of Australia's gliding possums, the greater glider (*Schoinobates volans*) is found in parts of Victoria, New South Wales and sub-tropical Queensland. North Queensland is inhabited by a slightly smaller sub-species, known as the northern greater glider (*Schoinobates volans minor*). This beautiful animal is quite common in open forests of the tablelands, wherever there is sufficient density of tall eucalypts. It has long and very soft fur; the upper-parts are basically grey, while the limbs are usually darker, almost black. Many northern individuals have a dark frontal and dorsal stripe, and the distal half of the long, woolly tail is blackish, only the very tip being bare-skinned. The under-parts are pale, but not white. The term, "dusky glider", suggested by David Fleay for the greater glider would suit the northern sub-species very well, for I have never seen any specimens with the striking white colouration on the head or body, which is apparently quite common in the southern species. The greater glider has a small, short-muzzled head surmounted by large rounded ears, distinctly fringed with fur. Illuminated by a spotlight, the eyes of a greater glider are more brilliantly reflective than those of any other possum, although the eyeshine of the lemuroid possum is nearly as bright.[6]

The northern greater glider is a very solitary animal. Only twice have I seen two adults feeding in the same tree, and the three dens I have watched house only one occupant, except in the case of a mother carrying a joey in her pouch. The solitary habits of the northern animal may be a specific character, not evident in the southern species, for David Fleay mentions that it is normal for a greater glider den to be shared by two animals and that when planing from one tree to another, the southern species frequently gives a gurgling call, probably intended to communicate its movements to its companion.[7] On the other hand, the northern sub-species seems to be quite non-vocal, even in the moment of capture.

The *Schoinobates* gliders are thought to have evolved from the ringtail possum group and, like them, these gliders appear to be strictly vegetarian. Their staple diet is provided by various eucalypt leaves, although they also lick nectar from gum blossoms. In captivity they accept jam, honey, chocolate and various fruits, but greater gliders do not thrive without the most careful and indulgent attention.

On one drizzly afternoon, during a heavy wet season some years ago, I set out to take myself and our dog for a walk. The route we chose ran alongside a barbed wire fence dividing two well timbered grazing paddocks. The dog attracted my attention to a drenched bundle of grey fur, suspended from the fence. Expecting to find a greater glider already dead, I was shocked to see the animal struggle weakly as I reached it. The poor glider was impaled through the tendons above one ankle and had twisted itself around the wire in its struggles. After I had unravelled the tangle, I held the limp wet body against my chest beneath my pullover, during the walk home.

I preheated the electric oven until it was fine and warm and put the glider in, snuggled in dry towels. At intervals through the late afternoon I switched the oven on briefly and opened the unlikely cage after dark. The glider jumped out immediately and ran across the room. I dived on it and Kay and I admired the furry animal, now dried out and much better groomed than it had been. Delighted with its recovery, I took it back to the area in which it had been found and set it on a big ironbark up which it climbed slowly, but without faltering.

Fences with a top strand of barbed wire regularly condemn the lovely gliders to a wretched death. The toll is particularly heavy where a new fence goes up across glider-inhabited country, and would largely be avoided if farmers would use plain wire for the top strand.

When Steve Parish, the National Parks and Wildlife Service photographer, visited the tablelands to obtain close-up portraits of possums, I joined John Winter and Rob Atherton in a successful attempt to capture a greater glider. We located one sitting in a tall stringybark; characteristically, it refused to budge despite our loudest shouts, banging on the tree trunk and so on. Eventually I volunteered to climb as high into the tree as possible, and then reach upwards with a ten metre pole we had with us. I struggled up slowly and raised the pole towards the glider, which now seemed to be on the verge of taking off. Luckily the pole struck the branch it was sitting on at just the right moment, so that the long glide it had planned got off to a bad start. The glider sailed along for about forty metres, steadily losing height until it fell lightly amongst clumps of tall soft grass. Everyone below rushed in pursuit, Steve in the lead and the spotlighters running behind, while I watched from above. Steve ran so fast that he outran the wavering spotlight beam and then overran the glider. Running in the dark he fetched up against a big tree, most of his breath knocked out by the collision. While he stood embracing the tree, the glider caught up to him and climbed the trunk, coming to a stop when it encountered his arms. Just then Rob Atherton rushed up and gleefully took the glider by the tail. While the ground party rejoiced over their catch, I was left to get down the tree in the dark.

The captive, a female, was kept in a soft cloth bag for the night, and she behaved beautifully in the studio next day. That evening I let her jump from my hands onto the tree where she had first been sighted.

Feathertail Glider

Should a possum-watcher become a little conceited, the tiniest of all the gliders will soon deflate his ego. This animal, the feathertail glider, is widespread in eastern Australia and may, in fact, be the commonest and most numerous glider in much of its range. Yet it is so tiny — smaller than a mouse — and usually so active, that finding one and then keeping it in sight for long are both very difficult. Through sheer luck my tally of feathertail glider sightings is probably better than average, but all my attempts to find a den occupied by these sprites have so far been in vain.

One night I spotted two feathertail gliders in the crown of a stringybark which was flowering out of season. I lay down on the ground and used binoculars to watch their scamperings amongst the blossoms for an hour, often losing either one or both animals for many minutes at a time, until their pale undersides were glimpsed once again as they ran or leapt about the foliage.

The feathertail glider is smaller than a mouse.

At home that night I set the alarm clock to make sure of waking up early, and was standing beneath the flowering stringybark by half past four the next morning. The masked spotlight showed me that there were still two feathertail gliders on the tree, and I hoped to be able to follow either one of them back to its den. I soon lost track of one, but still had the other glider in view a little after five o'clock.

Now, leaving a cluster of blossoms, it hopped from one branch out to the tip of another and from there sailed off the tree. Its glide carried it slowly, it seemed, across a distance of several metres to the trunk of a slender bloodwood. It ran up the tree to which I made my way as fast as I could, but that was the last I saw of the feathertail. I circled the tree, looking into the foliage from every angle, but all I saw was the blazing eyeshine of a greater glider, which further distracted me by taking off on a long journey of its own, swerving beautifully to avoid the crown of a casuarina in its path. I searched the surrounding trees for half an hour in vain. Before leaving I paced the distance over which I had seen the feathertail glide, and found that it had easily accomplished an aerial journey of twenty metres.[8] Although disappointed that I had not been able to follow the glider to its den, I went home with a valuable piece of information concerning its gliding ability, for until then the longest glide I had seen performed by a feathertail was eight metres.

That evening I went back to the same spot and stationed myself amongst the nearest, most likely den-trees. With the spotlight sweeping continually along the trunks and limbs of each of the trees around me I finally spied the tiny eyes of a small animal clinging amongst a tassel of leaves which hung down opposite a miniature spout. The animal remained motionless about twenty-five metres above the ground. Although I stared at it repeatedly through binoculars, I could not be sure of its identity. As it seemed in no hurry to move, I scanned the other trees at intervals, then swung the beam back to the animal I had already noticed. The longer it sat immobile the more likely it was to take off at any moment, so now I glued the binoculars to my eyes and stared until nearly dizzy. Eventually it moved just a little, and I saw it more plainly. A small tree frog. All that precious time lost in watching a tree frog. Jaded, I wandered along to the flowering stringybark and saw two nimble feathertails already amongst the flowers.

The following evening I changed my position a little, feeling that my chances were better, for now at least the tree frog would not mislead me. Bats took to the sky, two rufous rat-kangaroos bounced through the undergrowth, and a bandicoot rushed out of the bracken and sat on my foot. It seemed to know something was amiss as it squatted there — I was wearing shorts and sandals — but it was half a minute before it bolted back in the direction from which it had come. A huntsman spider ran down a tree trunk but I was not to be deceived by its tiny, brilliant eyes.

Then a flattish head with middling-bright eyes popped out of a "pipe" in one tree. I fastened on it hopefully. This could prove to be a feathertail glider peeping from its den. It stayed motionless while I quickly scanned other branches. I grinned knowingly at the tree frog which had just climbed from its retreat, and swung the beam back in order to watch the head showing from the "pipe". The animal put a front foot out, a flat wide-toed foot such as a feathertail has. Then it moved out still further and I saw it plainly. A gecko, unmistakably a gecko. Once again I slunk along to the blossoming stringybark and saw the feathertails already there ahead of me.

The next few nights were drizzly and the canopy was full of tiny, sparkling drops of water. This fruitless episode was by no means the first or last on which I have tried to trace feathertail gliders back to their den.

Some months before the same area had yielded other sightings of feathertail gliders. One night I saw two of them in a flowering bloodwood; one was feeding amongst the blossoms but the other was resting, head down, on a slanting limb not far above the ground. I watched it for many minutes. It was so completely still that eventually I was tempted into climbing the tree to find out just how it would react. I set the spotlight down so that it shone up at the feathertail, and began to climb. Although the slender tree shook quite noticeably, the glider took no notice of my ascent. Before long I was level with it and put my hand out to see if it could be caught, but the feathertail dodged nimbly aside, and easily evaded every subsequent dab, like a very agile mouse outwitting a clumsy cat. Finally it ran up the tree and joined the other feathertail amongst the blossoms.

There was to be another occasion when I saw a feathertail resting for a prolonged period. I had stopped to watch a greater

The feathertail glider seems to be a reckless and carefree adventurer.

glider, which had just landed on a tree trunk. It had remained motionless on the trunk after landing, while a brushtail possum stared at it from a perch on a nearby sapling. When the brushtail leapt across to the tree the greater glider ran upwards. Immediately after, a feathertail glider struck the tree, just above the brushtail; disturbed by the brushtail, it ran to the end of a short limb and threw itself off the end without seeming to care in the least where it would land. It fell onto a lantana stem reaching upward from a big clump. In the next instant it leaped agin, quite as uncaringly. I saw it lower down in the clump running about for a moment, and then it settled, head down on a stem, motionless. After watching it for about ten minutes, I noticed a common ringtail possum carrying twin joeys on its back a few metres away, and went off to watch them.

The feathertail glider often seems to throw itself off from wherever it is, little concerned about its destination. The most comic instance of this occurred one night when I was watching a much larger glider feeding on the sap of a big stringybark. I had seen feathertails feeding at this tree in the past and was half expecting their arrival. Suddenly one sailed into view and struck the bigger glider a glancing blow on its back. Had the bigger glider not been there, the feathertail would have missed the tree altogether. Now it swirled downwards and, by wheeling in the air, reached the tree it had been aiming for, but much lower down the trunk. It spurted up and fed on the sap for a while, then ran higher up the tree and leapt off, travelling towards a sapling eight metres away. When it struck this, it did not manage to hold fast, but fell off into the grass at the base of the tree.

Feathertails are elusive and, were it not for the fact that they are sometimes discovered during timber felling operations and can be kept fairly easily in captivity, very little would be known about them. John and Margaret Winter kept a pair for some time; the captives made themselves a nest of wood-shavings inside a small box supplied in their cage, and did well on a special diet made up from a Melbourne Zoo recipe.

These gliders lived in a large, glass-fronted box and the most surprising observation of their abilities was that they could spring to the pane of glass and not only cling there, but actually move sideways, or obliquely up or down. John Winter recalls that a glider clinging to the glass used to appear very closely pressed against it, the limbs of the animal being widely splayed. The feathertail glider has large pads beneath the tips of its toes; these pads have numerous fine grooves across their surfaces, which must provide sufficient traction for the gliders to grip on very smooth surfaces. Judging by their ability to cling to glass, it may be assumed that these gliders can walk onto a smooth leaf in search of insects, possibly including lerps and scale insects adhering to the leaves. Its extraordinary flattened tail is often curled lightly over a twig or leaf-blade to help steady its progress while foraging. Insects and nectar supply the staple diet.

A Mareeba naturalist, Kevin Sparks, once saw about forty of these tiny gliders thronging a flowering range bloodwood (*Eucalyptus abergiana*) in the hills east of Mareeba. He felt that this phenomenal gathering of the tiny animals was brought about by the fact that at the time of this visit, only one of the strongly scented mass-flowering trees was in full bloom and this had attracted feathertail gliders from some distance around. Together with his wife and a friend, he saw as many feathertail gliders in one night as most possum-watchers see in a lifetime.

Sugar Glider

With spotlight and binoculars beside me, I lay comfortably on the ground, my head pillowed on a log. The clear evening sky was traversed by a multitude of fruit-bats, most of which were flying past at a great height, although every now and then one came in much lower and could be heard settling in the foliage of the surrounding bloodwood trees which were in full bloom. A row of seven kookaburras occupied a slender branch, six of them packed shoulder to shoulder, while the seventh roosted a little apart from its neighbour.

It grew a little darker, the fruit-bats had their first squabbles and I switched on my masked spotlight, directing its beam at a point on a bloodwood limb, thirteen metres up, from which I expected to see a sugar glider emerge in the next few minutes. Passing this tree the night before, I had seen a pair of eyes glinting from a small hole. The onlooker had retreated and, knowing that I would do better with a red-masked spotlight, I moved on. At home next day I mentioned that I had probably found the den of a sugar glider and our son, Charlie, wanted to know if sugar gliders were really made from sugar.

A tiny pointed face appeared in silhouette, but was soon withdrawn. In a moment it peered out again, momentarily turned in my direction, and withdrew. There were many more cautious emergings and quick disappearings, sometimes due to the disturbances of a noisy fruit-bat, but more often by a stimulus I could not detect. Then suddenly, a sugar glider flashed right out of its den, its tail flicking and its body pirouetting so rapidly that it seemed as though the whole animal was spun about on a turntable. It launched itself in my direction, seeming to rise in the air for the first metre before it swooped down and settled on top of a casuarina.

A second head popped out of the den and went through its own series of appearances and alarms. It came out, ran up the branch, and then back to the den again, where a third face was already in view. The second sugar glider turned, ran up the limb and then out along a thin, dead branch. It ran faster and faster as it neared the tip and leapt off at such high speed that I could hardly keep it in sight, until it lost momentum towards the end of its glide.

Two sugar gliders were now peeping from the den, one head above the other. One withdrew and the other leapt directly from the mouth of its den, reaching a bloodwood sapling on which it ran up and down several times before crossing to a casuarina. A fourth inhabitant of the den followed the route of the first, landing on the casuarina which stood behind me. Once again it seemed to rise in the air at the beginning of its flight, so that I saw its white underside clearly before it began the downward swoop. When a sugar glider first peeps from its den, showing only a part of its head, its actions are so furtive that one is quite unprepared for the dashing animal which is due out.

I watched this den for several nights, never counting more than four tenants, and noticed that none of them followed a regular "flight path", for on some nights they all came my way, while at other times they dispersed in quite different directions, each following a route of its own.

The entrance to the sugar gliders' den was too small to admit my hand, so it seemed that the best way to examine the residents would be to saw off the hollow branch they occupied, in order to reach them from the rear. I explained my objective to three friends, all rock climbers, who accomplished the project one afternoon, while I looked on in comfortable idleness until the branch was lowered gently to the ground.

At the outset of the operation the mouth of the den had been plugged with a twist of rag. I left this in place now, while reaching into the hollow log from the sawn end. Once I had scratched away the powdery wood and frass in the hollow, my hand could sense the warmth imparted by the sugar gliders. Next I dislodged a few dried gum leaves, only a dozen or so, which had formed their scanty nest. I fully expected to have my fingers bitten as I delved amongst the cluster of furry little bodies, but only the largest male set to with a will as I transferred it to a soft pillowcase.

There were six sugar gliders in this den, two more than I had expected. Evidently, two must have slipped out each night while I followed the movements of one or another already abroad. There were three males, one of which was not yet fully grown, and three females. One of the females had two tiny joeys in her pouch; another was sub-adult, the unstained entrance to her pouch showing that she had never carried young ones. The colour pattern of the individuals varied in small details on the head and body. More noticeable differences occurred on the tails, some of which showed quite a lot of white at the tip, extending over more than two centimetres, while others had only a tiny dab of white, or none at all.

To capture this colony we had removed only a hollow limb, whereas zoologists or naturalists a generation ago would have had no qualms about felling the tree and hoping that the gliders would survive the crash. The colony, together with the den section of the limb, was transferred to our home. I pushed a discarded teddy bear into the hollow of the den log, so that it filled the space formerly occupied by the debris I had scratched out. The gliders' nest had been within twenty centimetres of the entrance and I made sure that they had at least as much space in the hollow as before.

This den log was set up in a biggish cage, in which I also suspended several short sections of quite large hollow logs and supplied four slender branches, on which the gliders could run the length and breadth of their cage. Sugar gliders have a hardy constitution, and my captives seemed to do well on a diet of eucalypt blossoms, honey, condensed milk and overripe apples during their three weeks in the cage after which I set them free. For the first week I did not disturb them at all, except for evening visits to replenish their food supplies. Over the following two weeks I spent several hours of each night sitting at one end of their

A sugar glider feasts on nectar from a variety of eucalypt flowers.

cage in order to learn something of their behaviour. They became fairly accustomed to my proximity, one nibbling my toe out of curiosity, and two others casually running over my body during their nightly activities.

The sugar gliders frequently entered one or another of the hollow logs during the night, between periods of feeding or exploratory activity. One night I watched four of them in a ball embracing, licking and nuzzling the others. The session lasted about one minute after which the participants parted amicably. On another occasion I watched one sugar glider licking and nuzzling another, which remained passive at the outset. The groomer directed its attentions towards it companion's ear, nuzzling vigorously at the base, the margin and inside the ear. Before long its already energetic actions became still more enthusiastic, the groomer straddling the other's body in order to hold it firmly. At this point the recipient rolled out from beneath the groomer and moved away.[9]

The only sound I heard from my captive sugar gliders was their characteristic stress call. Rob Atherton suggests that the continuous nature of this sound is caused by the glider's vocalizing during both the exhaled and inhaled breath. It is a strange, grating noise which seems to be used as a threat when a sugar glider is quarrelling with a conspecific, or frightened by any other animal. When I placed my ear close to the entrance of the den occupied by my captives, one of the residents usually responded with the threat call. Emanating from within the den, the sound resonates and is very like the buzzing of a hornet imprisoned in a bottle.

I once located a den through hearing this sound uttered repeatedly during a disagreement amongst the occupants. It was heard well after dark on a drizzly night, which had possibly caused the sugar gliders to stay in so late. At first the noise reached me indistinctly and I did not know what to make of it, but when it was repeated I decided to track it down. The sound led me to a tree which contained a den about six metres above ground. A month or two previously I had actually seen eyes shining from this hollow, but the animal had retreated. Now, with the calls as a clue, I masked my spotlight and waited determinedly until a sugar glider's head looked out. When the head was withdrawn the argument within the den resumed.

Since establishing the location of this den, I have spent many

A small hole in a tree can accommodate several lively sugar gliders.

hours standing near it, in order to watch a neighbouring tree in which I think there is a feathertail glider's den. Curiosity impels me to flash a masked spotlight at the sugar glider's den periodically, but I have never seen one leaving it; either they dash out when I am not looking, or they delay their departure until after I have left. Yet my frequent, activity-inhibiting visits have not caused them to move to another den, for I usually see at least one of them going home on my less frequent, pre-dawn visits to the area. In mid-winter I saw two of them carrying fresh eucalypt leaves into their den to add to the nest. The leaves, either singly, or in small sprigs, are nipped off while held in the paws, and transported in a curl of the tail. The number of leaves used is probably related to the population of the colony and the size of the den which must be padded out.

Although they use leaves for their nests, sugar gliders are not known to include leaves in their diet, which is chiefly comprised of insects, nectar and sap. In addition to these foods they probably kill nestling birds at times, for captive sugar gliders kept by David Fleay killed not only a small bird but also a mouse on one occasion. (Fleay, 1947.)

One night I disturbed a yellow robin from its roost in a lantana shrub. It flew hesitantly upward, alighting on a bloodwood limb. A sugar glider, which happened to be on the same limb, heard it approaching and ran along the limb as though to intercept the bird. When the yellow robin landed, the sugar glider had reached a point about three metres away, but now advanced no further. The glider's behaviour put me in mind of another incident in which a glider appeared to track by sound rather than by sight.

During the period in which I had kept the sugar gliders in a cage, I had put a small beetle in with them one night. From the reactions of one of the gliders it seemed to me that it followed the buzzing sound of the beetle more with its ears than its eyes. When the beetle flew erratically about, the glider's head weaved and bobbed up and down, both ears well forward. The beetle was roughly forty centimetres away, in a cage which was better illuminated than an outdoors, moonlit environment. As a sugar glider's eyes are set well to the front of its head, the exaggerated movements suggested that the beetle was being tracked by hearing rather than sight.

Various observers have recorded that moths, beetles, and

orthoptera, like stick insects and crickets, are preyed upon by sugar gliders, but perhaps not all arthropods are grist to their mill. I have watched one sugar glider carefully avoid contact with a big centipede which climbed up the tree which it occupied, and another which ignored several large ants which were feeding beside its nose where the sap oozed from a tree.

Nectar from a variety of eucalypt flowers is licked up, and sugar gliders also visit banksia and eugenia flowers. Kevin Sparks of Mareeba has seen these gliders at grevillea and hakea flowers and on the flowering spikes of grass-tree (*Xanthorrhea*).[10] Additional carbohydrates are obtained from sap-licking. I have watched sugar gliders spend more than an hour at a time licking sap which oozes from a big stringybark (*Eucalyptus resinifera*), where the bark has been incised by another, larger species of *Petaurus*. David Fleay (1947) mentions that these gliders chew on thin eucalypt branches in order to obtain the sap which they contain.

Sugar gliders are widely distributed in eastern Australia, occurring in both densely forested country and in drier areas, where the trees are more stunted and widely spaced. They must sometimes nest within the skirt of a grass-tree, for an acquaintance confessed that, as a boy, he had set fire to the mass of dead leaves which hangs beneath the crown of these trees, and had seen sugar gliders run out from them on more than one occasion. John Winter and I saw one glider visiting blossoms on a bumpy satinash (*Eugenia cormiflora*) in a rainforest, and he, together with Rob Atherton, have recorded sugar gliders in several northern rainforests.

These exquisite little animals are the smallest and most numerous of their genus, *Petaurus*. To see them amongst the trees at night engenders a fresh appreciation of our forests, and ever after, the sight of a small hole in a tree brings to mind the lively occupants which may be concealed within. Swift and bold, they are the Puck and Ariel of our bushland.

Fluffy Glider

Fluffy gliders are the most exciting and unusual possums I know. I first heard of them from John Winter who said they were probably in the district as there were records of specimens of this animal which had been collected in the 'thirties and 'forties. Then Percy

Tresize, author, painter and conservationist, mentioned seeing them on the Windsor Tablelands, further north, during a conversation we had with him at Laura. Finally, I became directly involved in a search for them when they were described by Jim Dawson, a resident of nearby Wondecla.

He asked if I had seen a big glider with "ears like a possum", meaning the brushtail possum. It had a habit, he said, of chewing into the bark of the big red mahogany or mountain stringybark trees which grew in some of the local forests. Guessing that Jim was referring to the fluffy glider, I questioned him eagerly. He suggested a few likely areas in which to search for them, adding that he and his brother had seen one or two of these gliders many years ago.

John Winter had by now moved to Townsville, but he and Margaret came up to the tablelands for the Christmas holidays in 1977. John described a big tree he had noticed on Herberton Range four years previously, which had carried numerous scars on its trunk. This sighting suggested the presence of fluffy gliders in the vicinity, for one of the foods these animals are dependent on is the sap of certain eucalyptus, which they obtain by incising the bark of the tree with their teeth.

At the time of his initial observation, John was mainly concerned with the occurrence and distribution of rainforest fauna, and had not taken up the search for fluffy gliders. Now, with him on holiday, the three of us, John, Margaret and I, made an impromptu decision to go out looking for fluffy gliders. John suggested an initial search in the area where he had seen the scarred tree.

That night found us walking amongst tall stringybarks, bloodwoods and turpentines, which towered over an understorey of marginal-rainforest species, with ferns and stinging trees growing thickly in the gullies. John stopped to point out a leaf-tailed gecko clinging to a turpentine, a rather unusual sight, as these geckoes are more often found in closed canopy forests. Just then a strange call reached us. John who had heard fluffy gliders in southern Queensland, felt sure that we had just heard one of these animals. We moved slowly into the forest. Almost immediately I saw a pair of eyes, but they proved to belong to a common ringtail. The call was repeated, coming from across a gully on our right and, almost immediately after, we heard a second call from some distance ahead.

The fluffy glider is a most exciting and unusual possum.

We waited quietly, but there were no more calls. John and Margaret set off across the gully in the hope of locating the first caller, while I kept to the bank, heading in the direction from which the more distant call had been heard. Scanning the pattern of tree trunks and foliage illuminated by the spotlight, I noticed a peculiar shadow on a horizontal casuarina limb. I had decided against bringing binoculars on this particular evening, as both my companions carried a pair. Now, separated from them, I had to stare closely at the shadow, about fifty metres away, before I could discern a dark bodied animal clinging to the branch; its head was turned away from me, and its tail was lying along the limb. After studying it for some minutes I staked my reputation by calling out to John that I had found a fluffy glider.

I could hear John and Margaret working their way towards me, and so could the animal. It stirred a little, and looked in the direction of the noise. It seemed a long time before John and Margaret neared the casuarina, guided by my light. Finally, John called out in confirmation of my guess that the animal was a fluffy glider. I persuaded them to come up to where I stood, as they would be able to see the glider in profile from my position. It did not move at first, though my friends actually walked beneath the tree it was resting on, but just as they nearly reached me it jumped to a big stringybark and slipped around the far side of the trunk. Too disappointed to speak, I stared after it wordlessly. Then, just as I was about to begin apologizing, the fluffy glider's head came into view, after which it circled round to our side, so that we saw it clearly.

It was a handsome animal, nearly as big as a greater glider, and strikingly marked. Its head was dark grey, the muzzle short and conical, tipped with a pink nose. Big pointed ears, looking almost white in the bright light, stood out prominently from its head, quite different to the rounded, fur-fringed ears of a greater glider. Running from its neck to the small of its back was a dark stripe, which contrasted with the brownish grey fur of the upper body. All four legs were black and a very noticeable black stripe ran obliquely down each thigh. The tail, particularly long furred and fluffy at the base, showed a diffuse dark stripe commencing at the base and widening progressively so that the last several centimetres were completely black.

We were roughly on the same level as the fluffy glider,

separated by the gully which John and Margaret had crossed. While one of us held a spotlight the other two stared through binoculars, remarking on its colouring, the big ears, the long tail and so on. John was making notes and diagrams of its appearance. While we watched, the glider began to bite at the bark of the tree, stabbing and tugging with its incisors until we could see the redness of the edges of a new incision. Another fluffy glider called twice, distinctly; the second call was answered by the animal we watched. Lifting its head it gave the peculiar call, which starts with fairly high pitched syllables and ends in a gruff chatter. "Skree-uk-skree-uk-wufa-wufa-wufa-wufa". The glider we were watching then returned to its sap licking and was still feeding when we left.

On the following afternoon we revisited the area in order to look more closely at the tree it had been feeding on. The tree, a mountain stringybark (*Eucalyptus resinifera*) has a very rough bark, in which the characteristic incision made by a fluffy glider is about five centimetres long and two and half centimetres wide. It is cut in the form of a shallow triangle, the apex of which points down the trunk. The incisions are not deeply gouged, penetrating only about one and a half centimetres to tap the carbohydrate-rich fluids carried from the crown of the tree down to the roots. Fresh incisions look as though they have been chiselled out at a shallow angle, while the callusing of old scars results in the bulging of the bark around the margins of the incision, so that the scar appears very much like a pair of human lips.

Only about half a dozen of the numerous stringybarks in the immediate vicinity carried scars.[11] The trunks of the trees most frequently visited take on a reddish appearance, partly because the outermost bark shreds away due to the glider traffic and also because the sap stains the bark a reddish colour. Scars can be seen as low as half a metre above ground and extend upwards to the point where the first branches lead away from the trunk, seldom occurring profusely above the main branches.

The terrain of the area in which our first fluffy glider had been found was too rough to permit easy spotlighting. Not only was the ground broken by a deep gully and strewn with big logs but there was also a profuse undergrowth, a good deal of which was comprised of very healthy stinging trees (*Dendrocnide moroides*), one of which I carelessly brushed against. I knew this fate would threaten me on night trips and resolved to examine other likely areas in more open country. Accordingly, after some time spent in exploration and photography of this memorable spot, we drove to another site south of Herberton where I knew the big stringybarks could be found.

Almost as soon as we entered stringybark habitat we found two scarred trees, one of which was quite heavily scarred. This was in open forest where the dominants were bloodwood (*Eucalyptus intermedia*), forest red gum (*E. tereticornis*) and turpentine (*Syncarpia gomulifera*) besides the stringybark which was of particular interest. The understorey was chiefly one of casuarina and acacia species with most of the ground pleasantly grassed except where patches of lantana had grown up. Quite a wide search of the area did not result in the discovery of any more scarred trees.

We visited the site that evening but although we saw the common ringtail and brushtail, as well as a few greater gliders, fluffy gliders were neither heard nor seen. A week later, after John and Margaret had returned to Townsville, I went back to the spot and was rewarded with an extended sighting of fluffy gliders.

Nearing the most used of the two scarred trees I could just make out a pair of fluffy gliders on the trunk while I was still about sixty metres off. These gliders have very weak eyeshine[12] and it was more through glimpsing their white throats and long dark tails that I became aware of their presence. They stared in my direction, twisting their heads this way and that in order to place my position from the sounds of my approach. Although I stopped about ten metres away, one of them scuttled upwards almost immediately and a pale shape shot away from the top of the trees.

The second fluffy glider remained on the stringybark, moving restlessly about at times, but always returning to the particular oozing incision at which I had first seen it. When it climbed down to this point from above I was reminded of a bat walking head down along the wall of a cave. This resemblance was occasioned both by the big ears and the posture of the body with head and shoulders held off the trunk by the bracing front feet, while the hindquarters pressed closely against the tree. When the glider climbed slowly upwards its movements were lizard-like, each foot reaching up after swinging outward in a short arc. As a consequence the animal moved sinuously, the resemblance to a lizard accentuated by the long tail.

While I watched the fluffy glider I deliberately moved about, lit my pipe and switched the spotlight on and off in the hope of accustoming it to my presence, for I planned to be back often, to learn as much about its behaviour as possible. Finally I retreated slowly while it continued to feed.

On my next visit, only one fluffy glider was feeding on the most used tree, its pink tongue shooting in and out with great rapidity. It did not stir when a loud clap of claws against the trunk announced the arrival of a second glider. The newcomer came into view a little higher up, very alert and almost jittery in its movements. Its large mobile ears were sometimes flexed so that they curved outwards at the tips. The long claws clinging to the bark were so polished that they sparkled in the light, and its throat and chest looked snow white. There was no form of greeting between the two animals when the newcomer took up a feeding position beside the other, yet it was clear that its presence was fully tolerated. The tails of the two animals were often in contact, and occasionally their haunches pressed up against one another. Both fluffy gliders appeared very nearly identical in size and colour, but the temperament of the second comer was more restless. It moved around the tree quite a bit after a few minutes of sap licking and then hopped rapidly up the trunk and high into the crown of the tree until it was lost to view.

A little later a flicker of movement lower down the trunk caught my attention. A feathertail glider was on the tree, its nose buried in a crevice of the bark. Then, with an abandoned flick of its tail it spurted up the tree and settled close beside the remaining fluffy glider, which was still feeding. For the next ten minutes the smallest of our gliders feasted on sap oozing from an incision provided by the largest *Petaurus*. Both animals clung head-down on the trunk, almost elbow to elbow. Abruptly the feathertail raced higher up the tree, turned about, and leapt wildly off. It struck a bloodwood eight metres away, glanced off and fell in the grass, after which I lost sight of it.

Next a sugar glider landed in a casuarina almost overhead. It swooped through the beam of the spotlight to land on a sapling near the scarred stringybark. Another leap and it was on the stringybark, running about on the trunk until it had found an oozing incision. As with the other gliders, this one too fed in a head-down position, probably to avoid the dribbles of sap which might otherwise fall on its fur. Some of the scars exude sap continuously for many weeks, day and night, a drop at a time trickling slowly down the trunk.

I had now seen three species of possum, all gliders, which fed on sap. On my next visit I was to see a fourth, a common brushtail, licking the oozing sap. This heavy bodied animal was not able to feed comfortably in a head-down position. The best it could manage was to approach the scar diagonally from below, in order to evade the sap. Two sugar gliders were feeding close by but there was no sign of a fluffy glider. Up in the first fork of the tree a carpet python was coiled, either resting or waiting in ambush. Normally an admirer of snakes, I was dismayed to see this one, for even though it was not a big snake I feared it might be large enough to engulf one of the fluffy gliders. It was in fact a long time before I was to see two fluffy gliders on this tree at the same time, but circumstances eventually acquitted the carpet python.

Although I saw feathertails, sugar gliders and the brushtail possum on almost every subsequent visit, sightings of the fluffy gliders were all too few. When I did see one it was either high in the foliage or it left the tree soon after I arrived. The second of the two scarred trees never showed signs of recent use and though I searched the area thoroughly I never saw any more scarred stringybarks. Recalling that one of the two fluffy gliders had always reacted to my presence with nervousness and remembering the carpet python, I pessimistically feared that the snake might have captured the more placid of the two fluffy gliders I had watched.

I had by now become very fond of this site; the area was rich with a variety of animal species. I had watched many bandicoots and rufous rat-kangaroos; grey kangaroos and agile wallabies had often crossed my path fearlessly and the trees supplied food to *Melomys* rats and a total of six resident species of possum. When the bloodwoods flowered they were thronged by hordes of fruit-bats. The heavily scarred stringybark was the source of so much bounty to so many visitors. In the daytime it was host to rainbow and scaly-breasted lorikeets, noisy miners and bridled honeyeaters which came for the sap. After dark large moths settled on the scars; feathertail gliders, not much larger than the moths, and three other species of possum came to it. Yet the fluffy gliders were eluding me too often and I decided to look for another site where they might be more numerous.

The discovery of the second site followed a talk with a local resident, Frank Wieland, who recognized my description of the scars to be seen on some mountain stringybarks. He told me that he had customarily referred to the scars as "gum marks" but had not known that a glider was responsible for their occurrence. Frank described the location of a particular scarred tree growing in the state forest where he had a cattle grazing lease.

Guided by his directions I found the tree and, while exploring the area, discovered several more scarred stringybarks. There were five trees which appeared to be regularly used and at least that number again showing old scars. All the trees stood within a half-hectare patch of gently sloping ground. The dominant trees were flooded gum (*Eucalyptus grandis*) and stringybark along with a few bloodwoods and turpentines. The chief understorey trees were casuarina, with only a light shrub layer. Ferns constituted much of the ground cover, with soft grass and native violets plentiful where ferns did not dominate. A gully just beyond the site sheltered many marginal rainforest species and on this first visit I startled a brush turkey and was surprised to see a Lumholtz's tree kangaroo resting in a casuarina which leaned out over the gully. Further south, beyond the gully, the forest thinned out markedly; in fact the half-hectare patch containing the scarred stringybarks was the most densely forested area for a kilometre or so in any direction.

On my first evening visit in 1978, I made sure of arriving well before dark in the hope of hearing the fluffy gliders call when they first emerged from their dens. I sat against a log, facing the western sky, against which the crowns of several big trees were silhouetted. As the light faded on this January evening, the cicadas set up a tremendous shrilling and I resigned myself to being able to hear nothing while their din lasted. Then a fluffy glider call rang out above their noise and was immediately followed by another. Spotlighting had to wait until the evening grew darker, but hearing the gliders so clearly was delightful. Watching the sky and the pattern of branches against it, I saw a movement on a broken limb jutting from a tall flooded gum. A fluffy glider ran along the branch and turned up an arching offshoot. I saw it swooping away from the branch, actually banking as it sped between the trees. Very soon after, a second fluffy glider climbed from the broken end of the branch on which the first had appeared. Evidently the branch was hollow and contained a den. The second glider followed the path taken by the first one, but I did not see it glide away. It was now almost dark, and the voices of several fluffy gliders could be heard at frequent intervals. As the animals are highly mobile, and each one might be calling from the successive points it moved to, I could be certain of no more than three individuals calling from widely separated points in the forest. Although I was using a bright spotlight and wandered among the trees for a long time, I did not, at first, see any fluffy gliders. The trees were very tall and, knowing how weak the eyeshine of these animals is, I concentrated my efforts on the trunks of the trees, but to no avail, until I was about to leave.

Then the sound of claws on bark caused me to flash the spotlight along the trunk of a bloodwood tree. I saw one fluffy glider about five metres up, climbing slowly higher, and could see the tail of another, which was otherwise out of sight on the far side of the tree. It then came fully into view, and both animals moved slowly upwards. The leading animal continually delayed the other's progress by walking across its path, sometimes actually climbing over its companion's head. Occasionally the obstructive glider mouthed the fur of the other's shoulders. Both animals circled the tree trunk and were lost to view. I waited for some time, hoping to see them return to my side of the tree. I could still hear their claws, intermittently, on the bark; finally I worked my way quietly around to the far side of the tree. The fluffy gliders were mating.

The female was clinging to the underside of a branch, where it forked out from the trunk. The male had almost enveloped her; his front feet clasped her shoulders, while his hind feet were spread widely, one beside each of hers, clinging to the bark of the tree. The long tails of the animals swayed and twirled about, sometimes entwined together. Occasionally their grip on the tree slipped slightly, dislodging small flakes of bark which floated down. Minutes passed, another fluffy glider called from a nearby tree, but the pair I watched made no vocal noise. Suddenly both of them lost their hold on the tree and fell. They parted and each rolled over in the air, to land lightly side by side on a casuarina limb two metres lower down. They crossed back to the bloodwood and went slowly up again, the female making no effort to evade its mate, which followed closely. One of them called now, just once.

They moved slowly higher and were lost to view. Feeling extraordinarily lucky to have watched this incident, I made no attempt to relocate them.

My thoughts went back to another place, where I had encountered two shingleback lizards mating on an arid sandhill in the outback. That had been a symbol of vitality in the midst of a harsh environment. Here it was the pairing of two soft and lovely creatures in a fertile forest.

John chanced to come up from Townsville on the following day, and I told him about the new site which I named the "Forest Colony" to distinguish it from the other site I had been visiting, which I called the "Kino Tree".[13] We went out to the "Forest Colony" that evening, and John sat closer to the den I had located the previous night. It was a heavily overcast and drizzly evening. The cicadas cancelled their performance and only two or three fluffy glider calls were heard. I sat in another part of the forest until dark, in the hope of locating a second den, and later roamed amongst the trees with a spotlight. When I rejoined John he reported seeing either three or four fluffy gliders emerge from the den, but remarked that all of them had behaved timidly when confronted by the beam of the spotlight. Some of them had run back into the den, which had made it difficult to keep a tally. Later John had seen fluffy gliders on a scarred stringybark, but they had soon moved off. My own spotlighting had yielded no sightings. Plagued by leeches and damp, we left early, content with having come out so that John should know the location of the "Forest Colony" site.

Prompted by John's remark about the apparent light-shy reactions of the fluffy gliders, I carried a masked spotlight on my next visit two days later. I waited for dark at the spot from which I had seen the gliders leave their den on my first evening at the "Forest Colony". The overcast sky let down a heavy shower just after the first fluffy glider emerged. Neither it, nor the second glider, which came out after the shower, called as they set off from the tree.

A third fluffy glider, evidently arriving from a different den, alighted on a stringybark very close to me. It ripped at the bark for a moment and then went higher to launch itself. A fourth glided past me, not far overhead, and landed in a big bloodwood. It climbed the trunk and detoured out over a short, dead branch. It chewed on the end of this branch, sat on it for a moment and then returned to the trunk, up which it went with a few flaunting jerks of the tail. None of these gliders had called. Their calling is certainly not compulsive in the sense that a particular action is always proceded, accompanied, or followed by a call, and a call by any one glider is not necessarily answered by any other in the vicinity.

Setting off to tour the scarred trees, a sugar glider overtook me and landed on one of them. A fluffy glider was already at the tree, ripping bark from the trunk. It seemed unconcerned by my approach, so I went very close, until the fluffy glider was no more than three and a half metres away, with the sugar glider a metre or so higher.

The fluffy glider went up, met the sugar glider and chased it for a few paces. I saw a second fluffy glider starting down the tree, as the first one circled to the far side of the trunk. I followed the first glider around the tree, where it was once again ripping at the bark as though to make a feeding incision.

Next it began to groom itself. Releasing the hold of its front feet, it leaned back from the tree and twisted to grasp a hip with the front foot of the same side. Now, reaching around as far as possible, it began to mouth the fur of its back. When it resumed a hold on the tree with one front paw, it let go a hind foot, with which it began to scratch very rapidly at the base of its tail. Finally, hanging by one front foot alone, the glider swung from the tree, its body turned side-on to the trunk. Thrusting one hind leg out rigidly, it scratched along the entire length of this limb with the claws of the other hind foot.

This manoeuvre, accomplished with the greatest of ease, terminated the grooming session. Meanwhile, the other fluffy glider had come around to my side of the tree and stopped about a metre above the one which had been grooming. The second comer stared down, sniffed hard and made short, lunging motions with its body, though without moving its feet. Its actions resembled those of a dog inciting another dog to play. The first fluffy glider took no notice; the newcomer turned and hopped back up the tree, calling once as it went.

While leaving the area that night I heard the crash of a landing in the foliage of a tree. The masked spotlight showed a fluffy glider clinging to the twiggy ends of a flooded gum branch. It appeared to be ripping at the bark of the twigs, but I could not determine whether this resulted in its obtaining any food. After a few minutes the glider hung upside down from the twigs and began to groom. Hanging by the hind legs alone, it took its tail in its front paws and passed the distal end through its mouth. It licked and scratched for a long time, but with drizzle-fogged binoculars and a masked spotlight, many of the details of its actions evaded me. Despite the decreased visibility resulting from a masked spotlight, I felt that its use had been most worthwhile, for all the gliders I had sighted on this visit had seemed oblivious of the red light.

I was so delighted by the density of the fluffy glider population in this tiny area that I decided to visit the Atherton offices of the State Forestry Department and call on Dave Cassells, an officer with whom I was already quite well acquainted. To him I described our rediscovery of fluffy gliders in the district and the appearance of the scarred stringybarks. I mentioned the area Frank Wieland had directed me to and asked Dave if he could ensure its protection from the logging operations.

Dave proposed that we go out together so that he could see the trees in question. Not many days later we went to the "Forest Colony" site in daylight, and I pointed out the scarred trees while we strolled through the area. Dave said that it should be quite possible to secure protection for the area under the classification of a Scientific Purposes Reserve, considering the dense population of fluffy gliders it supported. We set a date on which to come out spotlighting together, in order that Dave should see the fluffy gliders.

As we drove out on the appointed evening, Dave had a story to tell. That very morning a timber cutter from Ravenshoe had telephoned him, as the local forester was out of town. The timber cutter told Dave that he had been allotted a sale of logs covering the area in which the "Forest Colony" was situated, and wished to have them marked as he wanted to begin felling operations. Had the Ravenshoe forester been available that day, this procedure would have gone ahead as a matter of course. Dave explained that the particular site was of interest because of the fluffy glider colony and requested that the timber cutter accept a sale of trees in another area. The near disaster to the "Forest Colony", and its lucky reprieve, was underscored by the fact that it would have been stringybarks which would have been felled, in order to favour the regeneration of flooded gums in the area.

The fluffy gliders gave us a grand performance that night. We sat at the spot from which the den in the flooded gum could be watched. It was a heavily overcast evening with a very light drizzle. White-kneed crickets and tiny frogs sent up a louder chorus than the cicadas. The first fluffy glider climbed out and ran along its accustomed path. Dave missed seeing this one, but I switched on a masked spotlight in time for him to see the next resident come out.

Just after this, three fluffy gliders planed across in rapid succession, almost overhead. All of them landed on a big bloodwood to our left. This tree has a small, dead branch, about half a metre long, jutting from the trunk. On a previous occasion when a fluffy glider had landed on this tree, I had watched it detour out over this stump on its way up the tree. It had chewed at the jagged end and sat on the stub before going on. Now two of the fluffy gliders repeated this behaviour, the first one fairly thoroughly and the second cursorily. It occurred to me that the animals may have been marking the stub with scent.

I glanced back at the den tree just in time to see a third fluffy glider emerge. This established that there were at least six of these animals in the "Forest Colony". Two of those which had been on the bloodwood now glided back, again passing close by us, unperturbed by the red light which tracked them.

We saw no more fluffy gliders that night, but sighted a brushtail, a ringtail and a greater glider on the way out. I think Dave felt well rewarded for his effort, while I was immensely gratified by his interest and the protection gained for the "Forest Colony".

On the occasion of John Winter's first visit to the "Forest Colony" site, we had detoured via the "Kino Tree' site on our way home. There we had watched a fluffy glider feeding, carefully illuminating it with only the side glow of our spotlights in order to avoid frightening it. Wanting to examine it closely, measure it and take some close-up photographs, we thought of a way to catch it. Our whispered plans were quickly put into action and soon the fluffy glider was in our hands, quite unhurt and too surprised to be aggressive. It proved to be a female with a very small joey in her pouch. The female measured a total of 71.2 centimetres, of which her tail accounted for 43.2 centimetres. I photographed her on the following day and kept her for a week while the films were away being processed. I gave her masses of gum blossoms and, following David Fleay's experience, supplied her with melon and lemon jam, honey and bread soaked in sugared milk. She was most partial to the melon jam, but ate very small quantities; I could not judge how far she availed herself of the gum blossom nectar.

I was too anxious about her well-being to risk disturbing her by trying to make any observations on behaviour. When I replenished her food supply each evening, I made a check of the cage to see if she had cast her joey from her pouch, a shock reaction to which many marsupials are subject, but was relieved to find nothing. As soon as I heard that the photographs were adequate, Kay and I and our two boys set off for the "Kino Tree" at dusk. Just before I released the fluffy glider I made sure that the joey was still in her pouch. Thankful that this was so, I set the glider on her feeding tree, up which she sped at top speed.

Although I saw a brushtail and one or two sugar gliders feeding on the sap of the "Kino Tree" on most subsequent visits, it was several months before any fluffy glider stayed at the tree for more than a few minutes after I arrived, even though I always carried a masked spotlight. I used to smile wryly at the timidity of the fluffy gliders, wondering if it were the female, our one-time captive, which I had glimpsed, or the other animal, which I had sometimes sighted here and which had always been light-shy.

That the second fluffy glider at the "Kino Tree" site was a male could be assumed from the fact that the female we had examined had been successfully impregnated. The presence of an adult male was established some months later, under tragic circumstances. Kay and the boys had come with me to the "Kino Tree" site for an afternoon stroll and were walking some distance ahead when Kay came running back, calling out that a fluffy glider was caught on the fence.

We found that both its gliding membranes had been impaled on barbed wire, and the tip of its tail was also snagged on the fence. The glider was still alive and alert, although hanging helplessly in a pitiful tangle. I unsnagged its tail and prised one of its membranes off a prong of the barbed wire. The glider made no effort to bite as Kay held it while I tried to release the other membrane. The animal must have spun around the wire after it had first struck the fence, originally impaled through only one membrane. Now we had to pass it right around the wire in the opposite direction before it was free.

Kay held it while I examined the torn membranes on which flies had deposited myriads of eggs. Both of us were in a quandary as to what it would be best to do. When we first saw the plight it was in we had thought of killing it as quickly as possible, but when the poor, bedraggled creature was in our hands we knew that we could not do it. The choice lay between taking it home to keep it while its wounds healed, or setting it free now. I felt that its efforts to escape from a cage would impair healing and that, as I would not be able to provide a natural diet, it might die in captivity regardless of our good intentions. Even were it to die from its wounds in the bush, it would at least be free and in familiar surroundings.

I placed it on the trunk of a big tree beyond the fence. It climbed strongly and went out along a thin branch, high above the ground, and began grooming. It did this while hanging beneath the branch in the characteristic manner of fluffy gliders, often using only its hind feet to cling to its support. When we passed beneath the tree half an hour later, the glider was perched on the same branch, its long tail swaying in the breeze. The weather had been overcast and drizzly for some days, much the same as it had been on the occasion when I found a greater glider caught on a fence. I wondered if the fluffy glider had been caught because of the poor visibility on the overcast night. I went back to the area after dark to see if it had fallen from the tree we had set it on, but there was no sign of it.

Nowadays there is an animal which comes to the "Kino Tree" from the direction in which the male had been found caught on the fence. I hope it is the fluffy glider which Kay and I had helped.

One evening in June a fluffy glider landed on the "Kino Tree" with a loud clash of claws, just after half-past six. I approached the tree after seven o'clock and saw a fluffy glider sitting on the lowest branch. Just then another fluffy glider planed in from further away, landing in the foliage of a tree which stood close to the kino tree. It called once, moved along towards the kino tree and began grooming. Meanwhile, the fluffy glider, already on the scarred tree, came down the trunk and began licking sap. The second comer called again and jumped into the foliage of the kino tree. It ran along the underside of a branch, all the way down to the junction with the trunk.

I saw that it was most unusually coloured, for its thighs and the region of the lower back were extremely pale, probably white, except that I was viewing it with a red light. The dorsal stripe ended higher up the back than usual and was poorly defined, but the dark stripe running diagonally down the thighs stood out very clearly. The neck and shoulders were dark, but blotchy rather than uniformly coloured, while the tail was of more or less standard colouration.[14]

I moved around the tree to follow the first fluffy glider. It was feeding on sap and took no particular notice of the pale backed animal when the latter came near it. Able to compare both animals, I saw that the newcomer was distinctly smaller than the other. Remembering the female and pouch joey which John Winter and I had captured at this site nearly six months before, I felt that the two animals I was now watching were the same female and her offspring.

The smaller, pale backed animal approached the other, making short, panting sounds and, once, uttering a brief call. It advanced to the larger animal and pushed through beneath its tail, resting in this position while the fully grown fluffy glider continued to feed. Shortly after, the adult moved a little higher up the tree and the smaller one took up the head-down feeding position at the oozing incision. The adult now turned about and came down to the smaller glider, thrust its head beneath the feeding animal's tail and pressed its forehead firmly against the cloacal region. While in this position, the adult wagged its head from side to side, pushing vigorously at the same time, so that the smaller glider's tail was pushed up vertically.

After this contact the adult fluffy glider moved a little to one side and took the smaller animal's tail in both its fore-paws to groom the distal portion in its mouth. This done, it again thrust its forehead against the other's cloaca as vigorously as before, while the recipient remained motionless throughout. Finally the adult pushed itself all the way under its companion to reach the sap on which the other had been feeding. The paler one, almost prised off by this manoeuvre, moved off to one side, only resuming its feeding when the adult had climbed up the tree.

This was the first social interaction involving bodily contact I had seen since the occasion when a mating pair had been observed towards the end of January. The animal with the pale hindquarters was also the only obvious sub-adult I had yet seen. I thought at the time that the interaction I had observed might have been an exchange between mother and joey, but soon I was to see the forehead-to-cloaca interaction occur many times between apparently adult animals; moreover, one animal sometimes took a turn as initiator immediately after having been the recipient of this unusual form of bodily contact.

On a visit to the "Forest Colony" in mid-June I sat under a group of large trees containing some likely looking "spouts", in the hope of discovering another fluffy glider den, but had no success. After several calls were heard and the full moon was well up, I walked amongst the trees and caught sight of a pair of eyes on one of the scarred stringybarks. Going closer, I saw it was a brushtail busily licking sap. While I stood near the tree looking up at the moonlit sky, I saw a fluffy glider planing between two big trees, calling loudly as it travelled. The usual call given by a fluffy glider while actually gliding is a loud, throaty gargle, but they will sometimes give the full call, beginning with a high-pitched "skree".[15] Almost immediately after it landed, it was followed through the sky by a second glider, also calling as it sped between the trees. The leading animal now glided to the scarred tree on which the brushtail was feeding, and I could hear it coming down on the far side of the trunk.

Next it appeared beneath the brushtail and climbed up towards the oozing incision which the brushtail still monopolized. The fluffy glider nosed at the possum's tail and then climbed higher, nudging gently beneath the brushtail's chest to try to reach the sap, but still the possum took no notice. That a brushtail possum, which is normally so insistent on an allowance of "elbow room" amongst conspecifics, should be so tolerant of the fluffy glider was most surprising to me.

The glider turned aside and rested, but just then a twig snapped beneath my foot as I shifted my weight, and the brushtail hurriedly climbed the tree. The fluffy glider began feeding and was soon joined by the second one, which I had seen following it earlier. The second glider appeared to lick at the sap which had already trickled down and dried, showing as a long stain running down the trunk.

A sugar glider arrived at the tree and licked sap from a smaller incision close by, undisturbed by the proximity of the larger glider,

Fluffy gliders are unusually active and restless towards the end of June.

even though one of these frequently brushed against its body while intent upon its own feeding. A third fluffy glider landed atop a nearby tree and called loudly, at which one of the two already on the scarred tree became agitated, climbed up and sped away. The third glider crossed to the feeding tree, came down the trunk and went directly to the animal which was still feeding. The newcomer thrust its head beneath the other's tail and rubbed its forehead against the other's cloaca. Immediately after, the animal which had been the recipient of this action circled around the newcomer and initiated a forehead-to-cloaca proceeding.[16] This done, it returned to its sap-licking, while the newcomer moved about restlessly, called several times and then left the tree. Several calls from other fluffy gliders in the area were heard during the time I was watching the interactions amongst those on the tree before me. During a short visit four nights later, when I brought a friend to see the fluffy gliders, we witnessed an almost exact repetition of the ceremonies just described.

The fluffy gliders seemed to be unusually active and restless towards the end of June, with a great deal of calling and moving about across considerable distances. On one night during this period I guided John and Margaret Winter and a third friend to a comfortable spot opposite the tree at which I had recently been watching. Leaving them at this spot, I went off to look and listen in other parts of the forest.

Repeated calling from some distance away guided me to an area I did not usually visit. Here the land rose quite steeply, and the trees were a little more scattered. The calling ceased when I reached the spot, but soon started up again, closer to the heart of the "Forest Colony" site. I stayed where I was and heard one fluffy glider giving an "in passage" call, which rapidly grew closer. The animal landed in a tree to my left, about eighty metres from where I stood, and called again. A moment later it glided past, overhead, and landed in a tree twenty metres to my right. Another fluffy glider was now approaching, calling as it moved, and took up a position somewhere on my left. The glider which had landed to my right now went off, and once again I could roughly track its movements by its calls, which indicated that it had re-entered the "Forest Colony" area. As I had not previously heard calls from this spot, I felt reasonably certain that both animals which had been here this time belonged to the "Forest Colony" and had, for reasons unknown, been travelling outside their usual home range.

My three friends had an entertaining evening, telling me, when I joined them later, that as many as four sugar gliders had been feeding on the tree at one time, and that they had seen three fluffy gliders in a row, all engaged in the forehead-to-cloaca interaction. Shortly before I rejoined them, a fourth fluffy glider had landed at the tree and was still there when I sat down to watch. This was the greatest number of fluffy gliders I had yet seen gathered on one tree at the same time.

One of them fed more or less continuously, clinging below the chief oozing incision in a restful position for which John suggested "papoose posture" as a descriptive term. In this posture, the hind feet of the glider cling to the tree at a point level with the mid-throat, while the front paws are advanced a little ahead of the nose. In this position the glider appears to sag against the tree, its hind end and tail pressed closely against the trunk. The "papoose posture" seems to be a very restful way of feeding at an incision; in fact a glider in this posture often seems to be nearly asleep, yet its fur will probably require extra grooming to deal with the sap which must adhere to it.

While one of the four fluffy gliders we watched scarcely stirred from its "papoose posture" and a second fed more or less persistently, the other two were mostly on the move because of one animal's repeated attempts to initiate a forehead-to-cloaca-interaction with the other. These two, one advancing and the other evading, made many journeys up and down the trunk and out along the branches. At one time we could see both of them hanging upside down from a branch, clasped belly to belly. They appeared to be wrestling lightly, although neither animal seemed to have any hostile intentions, and we were, in fact, not sure whether to regard their actions as wrestling or cuddling.

As the inhabitants of the "Forest Colony" appeared to be unusually active in the last weeks of June, with many social interactions occurring between various individuals, I decided to spend a full night out, watching at the tree on which the four fluffy gliders had recently been observed. Although our summertime observations suggested that the breeding season for these gliders coincides with the warmest months, it occurred to me that they might have a second breeding season, mid-winter.

I arrived early and made myself comfortable with an ideally

shaped rock for a pillow and my legs encased in a sleeping bag. Small bats were darting amongst the trees before the day birds were properly asleep, and an owlet-nightjar screeched repeatedly. A barking owl swept through the trees just before dark, and then a sugar glider landed on the scarred stringybark and began to feed at the chief incision on my side of the tree. Two more sugar gliders followed soon after and fed side by side on a smaller scar higher up the tree. A fourth sugar glider approached the tree from a different direction, and may have come from a different colony, for no sooner had it landed on the stringybark than the first arrival charged it. The two animals leapt at each other and both fell from the tree, grappling together. I could hear them struggling in the grass and mouthing a few grating epithets through clenched teeth. One animal, presumably the first arrival, ran back up the tree to the incision where it had been feeding, while the other climbed into a nearby casuarina.

Fluffy gliders were calling by now and one sped down from the tree behind me, to land low on the trunk of the stringybark. It hopped towards the chief incision and encountered the sugar glider which retreated momentarily, while the bigger animal commenced feeding. The sugar glider whizzed around and arrived alongside the fluffy glider's tail, where it began to lick the sap which had already oozed out. Comparing the two animals, I could see that the total length of the sugar glider was at least five centimetres shorter than just the tail of the fluffy glider. Once, when the sugar glider swivelled around, it trampled on the fluffy glider's tail, but the larger animal did no more than look around casually.

A second fluffy glider alighted in the crown of the stringybark and came down quickly. It approached the feeding fluffy glider without hesitation, and licked at the sap, the muzzles of the two animals in close contact. The new arrival then circled around, displaced the sugar glider, and briefly rubbed its forehead against the other fluffy glider's cloaca. Next it pushed itself between the other's hind legs and burrowed all the way beneath its body until it had reached the scar, where it began to feed. The first fluffy glider slipped off the other's back and moved around the trunk to an incision which I knew to be situated on the far side, just out of sight from where I watched. It must have chased a sugar glider from that position, for I saw the little glider race several metres up the tree, its white-tipped tail streaming behind.

The fluffy glider which had taken over the chief incision on my side of the tree was feeding contentedly in the "papoose posture" when it was approached by a sugar glider with a black-tipped tail. The fluffy glider made a threatening gesture, jerking a paw towards it as though to begin a pursuit. To my astonishment the sugar glider advanced with a small leap and made a loud sniffing noise. The fluffy glider pulled back a little, at which the smaller glider leapt forward again, sniffing aggressively two or three times. The fluffy glider moved away from the incision and was promptly succeeded by the little usurper, which defended its position successfully when the fluffy glider tried to return, repeating its short rushes and sniffing noises. Eventually it outdid itself. It leapt so vigorously at the fluffy glider, that it quite missed its footing and fell away from the tree until it wheeled in the air and re-alighted on the trunk about two metres lower down. Taking advantage of the situation, the fluffy glider regained its former feeding site.

As it turned out, it did not prove a grand night for watching interactions between fluffy gliders. Although there were three of them on the tree at one stage, only one was present throughout most of the night, while at about four in the morning there were none on the tree. I dozed at various periods through the night, waking at roughly hourly intervals to scan the tree.

A brushtail possum was feeding from the chief incision at four o'clock in the morning. It had come to the tree while I slept, but was not there for more than a minute after I awoke, for a sugar glider, probably the same one which had earlier driven a fluffy glider from the incision, now drove the brushtail away with similar tactics. The big possum retreated even more promptly than the fluffy glider had done, which made me wonder if a sugar glider often presses home its threats, or whether its aggressive initiatives were sufficient to frighten away much larger animals. It may be that the little gliders can inflict punishment but are themselves too agile to get caught, even though a bite from a larger possum would be more painful than that which a sugar glider's teeth could inflict. Even so, sugar gliders generally defer to the larger possums; perhaps it is only those with particularly robust personalities which bully their way into a feast which they have not had any part in providing.

A fluffy glider came down to feed at five o'clock and stayed for twenty minutes. It fed in the head-down position, pausing at times to stretch, by arching its back and spreading both front feet to their fullest extent, so that the dark-furred gliding membranes were exposed. When it climbed up to the crown of the tree it called once before sailing off. I heard a call from the vicinity of the den tree a few minutes later, and then a fan-tailed cuckoo called from the gully below. Soon after, while the sky was still dull and the trees looked black in the dawn light, a bridled honeyeater came to the stringybark.

A sugar glider going home.

Appendix A

Details of lengths of various possums described in the text.

These figures have been kindly supplied by Dr Michael Archer from data recorded by the Queensland Museum, Brisbane.

Species	Sex	Nose — Cloaca	Cloaca — Tail-tip
Common ringtail	M	323 mm	344 mm
	F	318 mm	331 mm
Green possum	M	352 mm	315 mm
	F	336 mm	319 mm
Herbert River	M	372 mm	354 mm
ringtail	F	358 mm	348 mm
Lemuroid possum	M	335 mm	316 mm
	F	337 mm	351 mm
Striped possum	F	256 mm	312 mm
Long-tailed pigmy	M	91 mm	130 mm
possum	F	78 mm	131 mm
Fluffy glider	M	266 mm	393 mm
	F	303 mm	430 mm
Sugar glider	M	155 mm	190 mm
	F	146 mm	182 mm
Squirrel glider	M	229 mm	241 mm
	F	193 mm	229 mm
Greater glider	M	398 mm	478 mm
	F	401 mm	474 mm
Feathertail glider	M	77 mm	72 mm
	F	67 mm	72 mm
Brushtail possum	M	418 mm	333 mm
	F	407 mm	315 mm

The squirrel glider is a species of *Petaurus*.

Appendix B

Squirrel Glider

Squirrel gliders (*Petaurus norfolcensis*) have been recorded from sites near Walkamin (Kevin Sparks), Watsonville (Ted Thomas) and Emu Creek (John Winter). These areas are not on the tablelands proper, the last two being west of the Divide, while Walkamin is situated in a region where the Divide is not a distinct geographic feature.

Following Ted Thomas' advice I made a spotlighting trip to Watsonville and sighted one squirrel glider which was caught in order to take photographs and measurements. The animal, a female, was noticeably larger than a sugar glider, with a much bushier tail, brighter eyeshine, and a paler face. It measured 47.3 cm overall, of which the tail was 27.5 cm. These measurements suggest that it was exceptionally large for a female, which are on average about 32 cm long, while males are around 47 cm in length.

Notes

1. Rob Atherton: Personal communication.
2. John Winter: Personal communication.
3. Thompson and Owen (1964) report finding unweaned joeys left alone during the day, in nests not occupied by their mother. They make no comment on when the young are collected by the mother. My observations suggest that they may be left unattended for a good part of the night.
4. Ted Thomas: Personal communication, and my own observations. See also Breeden (1970).
5. I once watched a green (ringtail) possum climb slowly but steadily up a strand of bricklayer's twine hanging from a beam.
6. Reflections of light originate from a specialized layer behind the retina of the eye. The purpose of this layer is to reflect back all the light received by the eye so that it passes through the retina not once but twice, activating the light sensitive cells in the retina on each traverse. Figuratively speaking, the animal gets a second look at each light ray entering the eye. This facility is important to a nocturnal animal seeking visual information from a dimly lit environment. The intensity of the "eyeshine" as it is loosely called, seems to be related to the excellence of nocturnal vision. Thus it may be supposed that the highly reflective eyes of a greater glider provide that animal with better night vision than a green possum has, while the brilliant eyeshine of a cat suggests that it has better vision after dark than any of the possums.
7. N. A. Wakefield in "Notes on the Glider-possum, *Petaurus australis*". *Vict. Naturalist* 87 (Aug. 1970), suggests that the greater glider does not call when abroad at night. He is of the opinion that David Fleay attributed some of the calls of the fluffy glider to the non-vocal greater glider.

    When I raised the matter with Mr Fleay on 20 July, 1978, he replied "regarding vocalization by the Greater Glider . . . . I still believe them responsible for gurgling calls 'in flight', though it is indisputable that they don't compare for noise with the fluffy species." See also Fleay (1947).
8. The gliding abilities of a feathertail glider seem to have been underestimated in Troughton (1954) who describes its glides as "prolonged leaps", while the *Australian Encyclopedia* states that these gliders can accomplish glides of one metre.

    Although the gliding membrane is diminutive, extending roughly from the elbow to thigh, I have observed several glides which traversed distances of more than eight metres, some of which brought the glider to a tree, while others — equally nonchalant — carried it down to the ground.

It seems to me that feathertail gliders can either make a swift direct traverse, or drift quite slowly, with the gliding membranes and tail fluttering slightly while aloft. Direction changing occurs most frequently during the slower speed glides.

9. The work of T. G. Schultze-Westrum (1965) with *Petaurus breviceps papuanus*, a New Guinea sub-species of sugar glider, has shown that adult members of each colony recognize each other by their body scent. Adult males have prominent scent glands on the forehead, the chest, and near the cloaca, while Schultze-Westrum believes that additional scent glands occur at the base of the ear and near the inner corner of the eye. Females have cloacal scent glands, and seasonally operative glands in the pouch, with which offspring are marked.

   Scent is imparted by mutual nuzzling and licking, with the dominant male of the colony actively imparting his scent to females and junior males, which also rub themselves against him in order to mark themselves with his scent.

10. Kevin Sparks: Personal communication.

11. It seems to me that the habitual use of a particular tree by more than one fluffy glider is in part due to the gregarious nature of this species, with particular trees serving as meeting places. When three or four fluffy gliders are at one tree (I have seen as many as five) some of them fail to secure a good feeding site, yet, even though they appear hungry and eager to feed, they do not leave the tree immediately. When they do leave I presume they go off to visit other feeding trees where fresh incisions ooze sap just as freely as those on the most used tree. Sap appears to be a staple for fluffy gliders at least in some months of the year, possibly when nectar or insects are in short supply.

12. If intensity of eyeshine is taken as an indication of excellence of nocturnal vision it is remarkable that fluffy glider's eyes reflect a light very weakly in comparison to those of a greater glider, although the former glides much more readily, and over quite as great distances.

   Even though the eyes of the sugar glider and feathertail glider are smaller than those of the fluffy glider, the eyeshine from both smaller gliders is actually brighter than that of the fluffy glider.

13. Some species of eucalypts, including the mountain stringybark, respond to bark injury by exuding an astringent liquid which dries to a resin-like material known as kino. Incisions made by fluffy gliders provide them with sap until such time as they are sealed over by kino, which adds to the reddened appearance of a frequently used tree.

14. When last seen at the end of September, 1978, three months after the first sighting of the pale sub-adult, it had grown noticeably larger and darker, although small whitish patches could still be seen on the rump and thighs. It will be interesting to discover if all fluffy glider juveniles are paler than the adults. No obviously sub-adult animals were sighted amongst members of the Forest Colony during 1978.

15. David Fleay mentions a "whirring moan" call given just before a fluffy glider planes from one tree to another (Fleay, 1947). To my ears this sound is very like the noise made by wind blowing across the mouth of a bottle.

The same moan precedes some of the full "Skree-uk-skree" calls of the fluffy glider, and the animals may use the full call or a throaty "Wufa-Wufa-Wufa" during a glide. Calling just before, during or upon the completion of a glide is no more habitual than calling on any other occasion.

16. Subsequent to the writing of the manuscript for "Spotlight on Possums" I have learned, through further observations on fluffy gliders, that this species has a scent gland located on the top of the head, in the area known as the "occipital region", namely where the skull and vertebral column are joined. This gland is more distinct in males, the site being usually marked by a thinning of the fur and the moist appearance of the secretion; though present in females it seems to be much less developed.

Close and repeated observation of the "forehead-to-cloaca" address has convinced me that the procedure is in fact a vigorous rubbing of the occipital scent gland against the underside of the root of the tail. The address is offered by females to one another, and to the male of their group, which also addresses females in the same manner, though often more casually.

Bibliography

Bolliger, A. 1944. The distinctive brown patch of sternal fur of Trichosurus vulpecula and its response to sex hormones. *Australian Journal of Science* 6: 181.

Breeden, S. and K. 1970. *A Natural History of Australia: 1. Tropical Queensland.* Sydney: Collins

Burton, M. and R. 1969. *The International Wildlife Encyclopedia.* London: B. P. C. Publishing Ltd.

Fleay, D. 1947. *Gliders of the Gum Trees.* Melbourne: Melbourne Bread and Cheese Club.

Jacobs, M. R. 1955. *Growth habits of the Eucalypts.* Canberra: Forestry and Timber Bureau.

Marsh, M. 1967. Ring-tailed Possums. *Australian Natural History* 15(9): 294-97.

Ride, W. D. L. 1970. *A guide to the Native Mammals of Australia.* Melbourne: Oxford University Press.

Schultze-Westrum, T. G. 1965. Intraspecific communication via scents in the gliding marsupial, *Petaurus breviceps papuanus.* Z. Vergleich. Physiol. 50: 151-222.

Thompson, J. A. and Owen, W. H. 1964. A field study of the Australian Ringtail Possum (*Pseudocheirus peregrinus*). Ecological Monographs 34 (Winter): 27 passim.

Troughton, E. 1954. *Furred animals of Australia.* 5th ed. Sydney: Angus & Robertson.

Van Dyck, S. 1978. *Destruction of Wild Tobacco Trees by Mountain Possums (Trichosurus caninus).* Brisbane: Queensland Museum.

Winter, J. W. W. 1976. The behaviour and social organisation of the Brushtail Possum (*Trichosurus vulpecula:* Kerr). Ph.D. thesis University of Queensland.